"Prompted by the question: 'what mi[ght] Christian traditions have to offer thos[e] [confronting] the complexity and uncertainty of our[...] Sheldrake has marshalled his vast kno[wledge...] well-considered, thought-provoking, a[...accessible...] Each section brings vividly to life texts, figures, artistic creations, and practices that both uncover the depth and breadth of classic Christian spiritual wisdom and illuminate the manner in which these gems can access a depth of human consciousness seldom plumbed in postmodern society opening a pathway both social and ethical toward an transforming encounter with sacred transcendence."

> — Wendy M. Wright
> Professor Emerita of Theology
> Creighton University

"Sheldrake makes the riches of the history of Christian spirituality accessible. By identifying five 'ways' or types of Christian spirituality, he captures the complexities, particularities, and evolutions of this history, as well as its cohesion. Ecumenically conversant and sensitive to contemporary context, this work will be valuable for the classroom and for the general reader."

> — Timothy H. Robinson
> Lunger Associate Professor of Spiritual Resources
> and Disciplines
> Brite Divinity School

"Are you looking for a contemporary text to introduce a class or group to the world of spirituality? You have found it here with this work of Philip Sheldrake. A master of the field, Dr. Sheldrake draws from his vast exploration into this topic to gift us with a text that is readable, informative, and wise. Clarifying the distinctions between spirituality and theology, he deftly offers the reader the necessary insight on how they nevertheless must interact. He offers the reader five lenses or types of spirituality while showing how they often interrelate in the lives of real people. A gifted writer offering wisdom on a hot topic, this is a jewel of a book!"

> — Carla Mae Streeter, OP
> Professor Emerita
> Aquinas Institute of Theology, St. Louis

"This is a must-read for anyone interested in spirituality! Sheldrake's historical exploration leads readers into an appreciation of spirituality as a multi-faceted diamond, which is not only a lived way of life and but is also a deep source of wisdom. Sheldrake invites us to interpret Christian spirituality through his lens of five ways/types: discipline, contemplation, action, beauty, and prophesy. These five ways make accessible the larger historical contexts that are critical for understanding spirituality today and being able to pass it on to the future generations. After reading Sheldrake's book I wonder how we question our own assumptions about Christian spirituality, and what communities can make that possible."

> — Laurie Cassidy, PhD, spiritual director and Christian
> social ethicist
> Faculty member of the Christian Spirituality Program,
> Creighton University

"Philip Sheldrake brings to a too-literal age the seer's gift for depth of insight, prophetic imagination, and the meaning of spiritual practice. The book will be a resource of value for teachers, practitioners, and writers for many years to come. Prepare yourself for a work of beauty and insight that reminds us that the Christian spiritual traditions are not lost. In fact, in Sheldrake's hands, traditions address contemporary questions and quests while remaining vibrant, animated, and alive."

> — Steven Chase, PhD
> Oblate School of Theology
> Editor-in-Chief of *Spiritus: Journal of the Society for the*
> *Study of Christian Spirituality*

The Spiritual Way

Classic Traditions
and
Contemporary Practice

Philip Sheldrake

LITURGICAL PRESS
ACADEMIC

Collegeville, Minnesota
www.litpress.org

Cover design by Susie Hayward.

1	2	3	4	5	6	7	8	9

Library of Congress Cataloging-in-Publication Data

Names: Sheldrake, Philip, author.
Title: The spiritual way : classic traditions and contemporary practice / Philip
    Sheldrake.
Description: Collegeville, Minnesota : Liturgical Press Academic, [2019] |
    Includes index.
Identifiers: LCCN 2019000315 (print) | LCCN 2019005654 (ebook) |
    ISBN 9780814644829 (eBook) | ISBN 9780814644584 (pbk.)
Subjects: LCSH: Spirituality—Christianity. | Spiritual life—Christianity.
Classification: LCC BV4501.3 (ebook) | LCC BV4501.3 .S5325 2019 (print) |
    DDC 248—dc23
LC record available at https://lccn.loc.gov/2019000315

To Susie

Contents

Preface

The theme of "spirituality" in the Christian tradition is extensive, varied, and rich. In the context of the current wide interest in spiritual wisdom, both among Christian readers and beyond, I had a desire to make the classic Christian spiritual traditions better known and more accessible to a contemporary audience.

Apart from writing, I have been teaching on the subject of spirituality for some thirty years in both academic and adult education contexts, on both sides of the Atlantic, to students from all corners of the world. I owe a great deal to the students and adults I have taught, and continue to teach, for the stimulation and challenges they provide. My own background is both academic and practical. I trained in the fields of history, theology, and philosophy and also studied in India for a year. Apart from teaching, I have worked in contexts of pastoral care, spiritual guidance, and interreligious dialogue. All of this has contributed enormously to the way I have come to understand and appreciate the riches of Christian spirituality.

I decided to focus this book on the concept of five distinctive "types" of Christian spirituality that I call the Way of Discipline, the Contemplative-Mystical Way, the Way of Practical Action, the Way of Beauty, and the Prophetic Way. In each case I have attempted to offer a broad overview of examples that show how these types of spiritual wisdom have been developed. However, in several chapters I have also highlighted one example that I feel expresses the particular style of spirituality in an especially rich way.

Finally, in my conclusion I have attempted to outline some aspects of the contemporary interest in spirituality and also to suggest how, in turn, each of the five types of Christian spiritual wisdom might engage with present-day concerns, problems, and challenges. In each case I have also offered a few thoughts on the kinds of spiritual practices that may enable us to deepen our engagement with the spiritual, ethical, and social values that are expressed in each type of spirituality.

I have been thinking about such a book for a number of years, but I am grateful to Hans Christoffersen at Liturgical Press for giving me the incentive to actually write the book. I was earlier given the opportunity to sketch out an initial summary of some of the ideas developed in this book in my essay "Christian Spirituality and Social Transformation" in the online Oxford Research Encyclopedia of Religion (2016). Thanks are also due to the Cambridge Theological Federation, where I am currently a senior research fellow at Westcott House, and to Oblate School of Theology in San Antonio, Texas, where I am a professor, for giving me the space and time to think, plan, and write.

As always, I dedicate this book to Susie, whose partnership, love, and insights have greatly assisted the book's development. In recent years Susie has also developed a creative role in imaginatively designing my book covers, and this is the fifth cover on which she has worked.

Philip Sheldrake
Cambridge and San Antonio, 2018

Introduction

The purpose of *The Spiritual Way* is to make the wisdom of Christian spirituality better known and more accessible to a contemporary readership. I will outline the ethos of a range of classic Christian spiritual traditions and how they might engage with the contemporary spiritual quest. In the context of the widespread interest in what is called "spirituality," both inside and outside conventional religious contexts, the approach I will take in this book involves, above all, a particular understanding of the notion of spirituality, especially as it relates to specifically Christian values and beliefs.

First of all, as I will explain briefly in chapter 1, the word *spirituality* is Christian in origin. I want to underline clearly that spirituality is not just a matter of cultivating spiritual practices or of achieving positive experiences and sustaining good feelings. Spirituality is, above all, a way of living according to certain principles and beliefs. Spirituality is also a journey. That is to say, spirituality involves a process of transformation that seeks to enable us to move from less adequate values and ways of life to what is more adequate and, indeed, fulfilling in an ultimate sense. In that context, all authentic forms of Christian spirituality point us toward what is more than the immediately satisfying or focused exclusively on the "here and now." Christian spiritual traditions all embody a sense of transcendence—the "beyond"—and point toward a final eternal endpoint for human existence. However, while Christian spirituality is undoubtedly concerned with the shaping and practice of human life, it also involves more than everyday practicalities and a framework of ethics. Authentic Christian spirituality includes some kind of vision that embraces a quest for ultimate meaning.

Types of Christian Spirituality

As this book will suggest, in relation to Christian spiritual traditions I have found it particularly helpful to identify a framework that is made up of major "types," or ways of understanding and practicing Christian spirituality. In different forms, these types of spiritual wisdom and practice are also present in the traditions of other world religions. Types or ways of spirituality are essentially distinctive styles of wisdom and practice that have some shared characteristics. In relation to such types it is then possible to develop a comparative framework (what is known as a typology) that enables us to explore the various styles of Christian spirituality and to understand the differences between them. However, we need to use such typologies with caution. While they are useful tools to help us understand the complexities of Christian spirituality throughout history, the notion of types and the ways of comparing them are interpretations of reality rather than straightforward descriptions.

In this book I will focus in particular on five types of spirituality, even though it is possible to identify a number of other types or ways. I call the five types of spirituality that I have chosen the Way of Discipline (expressed, for example, in ascetical-monastic traditions), the Contemplative-Mystical Way, the Way of Practical Action (expressed in classical "active" or mission-oriented approaches), the Way of Beauty (expressed, for example, in art, music, and literature), and finally, the Prophetic Way (expressed in, for example, political, liberationist, and feminist spiritualities). These five types sometimes overlap to some degree. For example, ascetical forms of spirituality may also have mystical elements. Each type tends to be characterized by a broad worldview, based on religious values. The different types of spirituality foster self-transcendence via a movement away from what they see as the "inauthentic" and toward what is deemed to be "authentic" in terms of a rich human existence. Broadly, in relation to spiritual growth, the inauthentic can be summed up as a sense of limitation or a lack of freedom. Each of the five types of Christian spirituality that I have chosen offers some sense of *where* spiritual transformation is thought to take place (the context), *how* it takes place (through which practices or disciplines), and *what* is the ultimate purpose or end point of the spiritual journey.

Before I proceed to explore my five chosen types, chapter 1 of this book, "What Is Christian Spirituality?," seeks to provide an introduction to the notion of spirituality in both general and Christian terms. First of all, where does the word come from? Then, what is the shape of contemporary understandings of spirituality, and why has the notion of spirituality become of increasing interest in our present times? Second, what is specific about the Christian approach to spirituality, and what are its scriptural roots? Chapter 1 moves on to examine the role of history in the study of spirituality, including the notion of historical periods and historical traditions. Overall Christian spirituality is then explored briefly in terms of the themes of transformation and of mission. Next, the chapter briefly explores the relationship between Christian spirituality and theology—both how theology helps us to evaluate the adequacy of various spiritual wisdom traditions and how an attention to spirituality enables us to move beyond a purely abstract and detached notion of theology to understand it better in relation to the Christian life and a Christian framework of values. Finally, chapter 1 briefly outlines certain fundamental characteristics of all forms of Christian spirituality founded upon the Christian gospels.

The remaining chapters then turn to my five chosen types of spirituality. The Way of Discipline (ascetical-monastic) sometimes prescribes special places, such as the wilderness or the monastery, as the preferred context for spiritual transformation. Characteristically, this type also promotes practices of self-denial, austerity, and abstention from worldly pleasures as the pathway to spiritual growth and moral perfection. The end in view is a condition of detachment from material existence as the pathway to eternal life. This type is explored in chapter 2 through attention to monasticism in its various forms, not least in the influential Western monastic Rule of St. Benedict.

The second type of spirituality, the Contemplative-Mystical Way, is associated with the desire for an immediacy of presence to God, frequently provoked through contemplative practice. It does not necessarily demand withdrawal from everyday life but suggests that the everyday may be transfigured into something wondrous. The mystical element does not need to be associated with extraordinary experiences, such as visions, but is more importantly linked to arriving at an intuitive (but obviously incomplete) "knowledge" of God that moves beyond discursive reasoning and analysis. The ultimate purpose of this type of spirituality is spiritual illumination and a sense of connection to the depths of human existence. This type of spirituality will be explored in chapter 3, which ends with an examination of the writings of the fourteenth-century English anchoress, mystic, and theologian Julian of Norwich.

The Way of Practical Action is my title for the third type of spirituality. This promotes everyday life in a variety of ways as the principal context for the spiritual journey and for our quest for authenticity. In this type of spirituality, we do not retreat from everyday existence and mundane concerns in order to reach spiritual truth or enlightenment. What is needed for spiritual growth is within our reach in our everyday lives. For, in the words of Jesus, "the kingdom of God is among you" (Luke 17:21). Because it emphasizes finding God in the midst of ordinary existence, this type of spirituality is in principle accessible to everyone and not simply to monastic or clerical elites or other special groups dedicated exclusively to the discipline of an ascetical life or with the opportunity for extensive contemplative practice. This third type of spirituality seeks spiritual growth through the medium of our ordinary experience, commitments, and activity—not least in service of our fellow human beings. This type will be explored and developed in chapter 4, which ends with a particular focus on the Ignatian tradition of spirituality.

The fourth type of spirituality, the Way of Beauty, is to my way of thinking often underestimated or even ignored in traditional studies of Christian spirituality. This type takes us beyond conventional written texts as the main source material for Christian spirituality. I would argue that the tradition of Christian spirituality is not limited to written material, but may include other elements that have some form of transformative potential. For example, aesthetics and art have a role in expressing spiritual wisdom. In particular, the Way of Beauty includes the creative arts, music, poetic literature, and architecture. This will be explored and developed in chapter 5, with reference to the great variety of aesthetic, artistic, musical, and literary expressions. However, I will give particular attention to three examples. First, the movement known as Impressionism, which has both artistic and musical forms, tends to step aside from overt religiosity. Nevertheless, Impressionism has a strong, albeit implicit, spiritual dimension. Second, the rich symbolism of medieval religious architecture has an overt spiritual message and significance, not least in the grandeur of Gothic cathedrals. Finally, in literary terms, the outstanding poetry of George Herbert, a major figure in seventeenth-century English literature who was also a priest in the Church of England, is a rich example of spirituality expressed through poetic literature.

Finally, my fifth type, which I call the Prophetic Way, goes beyond a straightforward engagement with everyday life and the practical service of other people as expressed, for example, in the Way of Practical Action. The Prophetic Way moves explicitly in the direction of a commitment to radical social action and social justice as a critical spiritual task. As we shall see, while it is possible to argue that historic spiritualities have always had prophetic or socially critical elements, an explicit attention to prophetic-critical spirituality and its development as a clear type only fully emerged during the last part of the twentieth century. This happened in response to a growing awareness of dysfunctional social and political situations that demanded some kind of radical action by way of response. Chapter 6 will make some reference to a range of political, feminist, and liberationist thought. However, particular attention will be given to the important liberationist spiritual and theological writings of the Peruvian priest and theologian Gustavo Gutiérrez.

In these five types of Christian spirituality, certain key themes will be noted. These include particular understandings of the spiritual journey; distinctive approaches to prayer and contemplation; the promotion of other spiritual practices; the role of spiritual guides; particular understandings of God, human nature, and human transformation; and approaches to practical action in the world. Importantly, all five types of Christian spirituality are, in different senses, ways of "knowing" beyond purely discursive, rational, intellectual, and abstract understandings of knowledge. The five types are also ways of "practice," or intentional ways of "being present in the world." All of them seek spiritual transformation directed toward the sacred and the transcendent, that is, God.

The conclusion to this book, apart from acting as a summary of the main features of the five types, will seek to draw out specific connections between each style of spirituality and the demands of contemporary human and Christian experience and practice, not least in a profoundly disrupted world.

CHAPTER ONE

What Is Christian Spirituality?

The origins of the concept of spirituality are explicitly Christian. Etymologically, the word derives from the Latin *spiritualitas*, associated with the adjective *spiritualis* (spiritual). These Latin words translate New Testament Greek concepts as they appear in St. Paul's letters—for example, the noun *pneuma*, or "spirit," and the adjective *pneumatikos*, "spiritual." In broad terms, it is important to note that in Paul's theology, *spirit* and *spiritual* are not the opposites of *physical*, *material*, or *bodily*, but rather the opposite of *fleshliness* (Greek *sarx*). This has a moral sense and refers to everything contrary to the Spirit of God. The intended contrast is between two vastly different approaches to life. A "spiritual person" (for example, as in 1 Cor 2:14-15) is simply someone within whom the Spirit of God dwells and who lives under its influence.

This theological and moral sense of *spiritual*, as "life in the Spirit," remained in constant use in the West until about the twelfth century, when, under the influence of newly recovered Greek philosophy, the concept began to be used as a way of distinguishing humanity from the rest of creation. Interestingly, during the Middle Ages the noun *spirituality* (*spiritualitas*) was most frequently used to refer to "the clergy." The word only reappeared in reference to "the spiritual life" in seventeenth-century France. However, this new usage was often associated with rarefied spiritual enthusiasms. Consequently, during the eighteenth and nineteenth centuries, other words, such as *devotion*, *perfection*, and *piety*, predominated in mainstream Roman Catholic,

Anglican, and Protestant Christianity in reference to a "spiritual life." The use of the concept of spirituality as a positive way of describing the spiritual life reestablished itself in the late nineteenth century and early twentieth century in French Roman Catholic writings. From there it gradually passed into English.

It was only by the Second Vatican Council in the early 1960s that the concept of spirituality began to replace older terms such as *ascetical theology, mystical theology*, or *spiritual theology*. The emergence of *spirituality* as the preferred term to describe "the Christian life" increased after the council until it became the dominant word from the 1970s onward, not only among Roman Catholics but also in Anglican and Protestant writings.

Contemporary Spirituality

Nowadays, the notion of spirituality is no longer confined to Christianity—or even to religion more broadly. Indeed, a fascination with spirituality, as frequently contrasted with institutional religion, is a striking feature of Western cultures in our times and is presumed to be accessible by everyone. In broad terms, how is contemporary spirituality defined? The answer is not simple because the word is used in such a wide range of contexts. However, current literature on spirituality regularly includes some or all of the following.

First, spirituality concerns a holistic or fully integrated approach to life. In this sense, rather than being thought of as simply one element among many in human life, spirituality is best understood as an integrating factor—attending to life as a whole. Second, spirituality expresses people's quest for the sacred. How is the "sacred" understood? The sacred in religious traditions such as Christian spirituality is based on beliefs about God. However, in wider society the word also refers to broader understandings of the numinous—for example, as embodied in nature or in the arts—to the fundamental depths of human existence, or to the boundless mysteries of the universe. Third, spirituality frequently embraces a search for meaning, especially the purpose of life, and for a sense of life direction. This association with meaning and purpose is in many ways a response to the decline of traditional religious and social authority, particularly in Western countries. Because of its association with meaning, contemporary spirituality implicitly embraces an understanding of human identity and of personality development. Spirituality is also regularly linked to a desire to obtain happiness or, more broadly, linked to the idea of "thriving." What does it mean for humans to thrive, and how do we come to thrive? Finally, contemporary approaches to spirituality often connect with the desire for ultimate values in contrast to a purely materialistic or pragmatic approach to life. Spirituality suggests a self-reflective life rather than an unexamined life and often overlaps with a moral vision.

These contemporary approaches to spirituality provoke some critical questions. First of all, is spirituality essentially a personal, even individualistic, matter or is it also inherently social? Interestingly, on the web, the majority of available definitions of spirituality emphasize inner experience, introspection, a subjective journey, personal well-being, inner harmony, or happiness. Here spirituality does not connect strongly with our social existence. This also provokes another question as to whether spirituality is more than another useful form of therapy—concerned with promoting everything that is comforting and consoling. In other words, can there be such a thing as "tough" spirituality that is capable of confronting the destructive side of human existence and action?

Some critical commentators on the contemporary phenomenon of spirituality are deeply skeptical about these developments. They suggest that the current enthusiasm for spirituality is nothing more than another version of consumerism.[1] There is some justification for this suspicion in a consumerist approach to "lifestyle spirituality" that promotes fitness, healthy living, and holistic well-being. However, in the new millennium there are already signs that the word *spirituality* is expanding beyond either an individualistic quest for self-realization or the search for satisfaction in life. The word increasingly appears in discussions about public values, the further development of professional fields, or the transformation of social structures. Some examples are spirituality in reference to health care, to the nature of education, to business and economics, to the arts, and, more recently, to the re-enchantment of cities and urban life. There is even

---

[1] See Jeremy Carrette and Richard King, *Selling Spirituality: The Silent Takeover of Religion* (London: Routledge, 2004).

some suggestion that we desperately need to recover a sense of the spiritual in politics. Academically, spirituality has now begun to appear in disciplines well beyond the confines of theology or religious studies, such as philosophy, psychology, and the social sciences.[2] This means that even a specialist area of study such as Christian spirituality must take note of many disciplines, methodologies, and areas of practice.[3]

Why Spirituality?

The contemporary interest in spirituality, particularly in Western countries, is part of a broader process of cultural change during the late twentieth century. For a range of reasons, our inherited religious and social identities, as well as our value systems, have been seriously questioned. As a result, many people in the northern hemisphere no longer see traditional religion as an adequate channel for their spiritual aspirations and look for new sources of self-orientation. Spirituality has become an alternative way of exploring the deepest self and the ultimate purpose of life. Overall, the spiritual quest has increasingly moved away from outer-directed authority (for example, in the church) to inner-directed experience, which is seen as more reliable. This subjective turn in Western culture has created a diverse approach to spiritual experience and practice. Nowadays, spirituality is frequently eclectic and mixed, drawing as it does from different religious traditions as well as from popular psychology.

People who no longer call themselves "religious" often describe themselves as "spiritual." They express this in the values they espouse and the practices they undertake to pursue a meaningful life. One British research project illustrates this. Sociologists Paul Heelas and Linda Woodhead, in the Department of Religious Studies at Lancaster University, have written extensively on religion and spirituality in the modern world. In their book *The Spiritual Revolution:*

---

[2] The magisterial work of Kees Waaijman, *Spirituality: Forms, Foundations, Methods* (Leuven, Belgium: Peeters, 2002), explores the breadth of the new academic field.

[3] On the increasing variety of disciplines and definitions in relation to spirituality, see Peter Holmes, "Spirituality: Some Disciplinary Perspectives," in *A Sociology of Spirituality*, ed. Kieran Flanagan and Peter Jupp (Aldershot, UK: Ashgate, 2007), 23–41.

Why Religion is Giving Way to Spirituality, they describe their research into contemporary religious and spiritual attitudes in northern England. They then compare their findings with evidence from wider Europe and from the United States. Heelas and Woodhead conclude that what they call "holistic spirituality" is gradually replacing religion in an evolutionary development because it was a better fit with contemporary needs. Although the book was published in 2005, its broad conclusions about the ascendancy of spirituality over conventional religion appear to have stood the test of time.[4]

However, one problem with the evolutionary aspect of this interpretation is that it operates within very specific boundaries. If the study of history teaches us anything, it is that making too many definitive assumptions about a complete rupture with the past, in this case a religious past, is a risky move. Even the ways we perceive the present moment are ambiguous. While, in terms of Western societies, it is true that increasing numbers of people in nontraditional settings explore a diversity of spiritual theories, experiences, and practices, it is also true that other, often young and intelligent, people are converting to very conservative forms of religion, such as Christianity or Islam, as their answer to the problem of ultimate meaning in what they experience as a confusing and dangerous world. If we move beyond the narrow confines of Western countries and take into account Asia, Africa, and Latin America, assessments of the definitive death of conventional religion are even more questionable.

Thinking of people in Western countries who continue to identify with Christianity, it is clear that many of them are also increasingly adopting a mixture of spiritual wisdom and are borrowing from across the boundaries of both spiritual traditions and religious faiths. Thus, many Christians are fascinated with Buddhist philosophy and practices, such as mindfulness meditation. Back in 2007, Dutch social anthropologist Peter Versteeg analyzed the work of Catholic spirituality centers in the Netherlands. These had created an interesting place for themselves on the religious-spiritual landscape, situated somewhere between the institutional church and the world of alternative spiritualities. The qualifying adjective *Catholic* often referred

---

[4] See Paul Heelas and Linda Woodhead, *The Spiritual Revolution: Why Religion is Giving Way to Spirituality* (Oxford: Wiley-Blackwell, 2005).

only to the fact that such centers had a Christian origin. What was on offer, and often continues to be, is frequently identified simply as "spirituality" without any explicit reference to Christian belief.[5] A similar eclecticism can be detected in the programs of many Christian retreat houses and spirituality centers of different denominations throughout the Western world.

This approach to spirituality among contemporary Christians raises complicated questions about how we are to understand the way a religious tradition like Christianity functions in radically plural contexts. A French social scientist and expert on Islam, Olivier Roy, borrowed the word *formatage,* or "formatting," from computer language in his 2007 analysis of the process whereby religions and their spiritual traditions are "reformatted" to fit the norms of the plural cultures within which they exist.[6] This reformatting may occasionally be "from above" when religious authorities consciously try to adapt to new cultural-social realities. However, reformatting is more likely to be "from below." Here, in informal ways, and sometimes in contrast to the attitudes of religious authorities, classic religious themes are reformulated, spiritual practices are adapted, or new ways of life are adopted to reexpress a tradition. In Christian terms, something crucial remains identifiably "Catholic," "Anglican," or "Lutheran," for example, or "Benedictine," "Carmelite," or "Ignatian." Yet, at the same time, fundamental ways of understanding such designations and their expressions change in significant ways.

What Is Christian Spirituality?

In the twenty-first century we are increasingly conscious of existing in a globalized and radically plural world. In such a context, Christian spirituality is nowadays explicitly situated within a world of many religions. One result is that Christian spirituality has become an important element in the critical dialogue between religious faiths—for example, between Christianity and Islam.

---

[5] Peter Versteeg, "Spirituality on the Margins of the Church: Christian Spiritual Centres in the Netherlands," in *A Sociology of Spirituality*, ed. Flanagan and Jupp, 101–14.

[6] See, for example, Olivier Roy, *Secularism Confronts Islam* (New York: Columbia University Press, 2007).

However, the contemporary taste for eclecticism raises some new questions about the uniqueness or otherwise of Christian spirituality. There are clearly overlaps between the values and concerns of religious spiritualities. All of them are based on a framework of transcendent beliefs, whether these are explicitly theistic (as in the Abrahamic family of faiths) or not (as in Buddhism, for example). Religious spiritualities also share other characteristics, such as foundational scriptures, some visible structures, sacred spaces, and spiritual practices. Yet each religious tradition is clearly distinctive.

Thus, Christian spirituality has a quite particular flavor and content. Indeed, as already noted, Christianity is the original source of the word *spirituality*, although it has now passed into other faith traditions, not least such Eastern religions as Buddhism and Hinduism.[7] In Christian terms, spirituality refers to the way our fundamental values, lifestyles, and spiritual practices reflect particular understandings of God, human identity, and the material world as the context for human transformation.

The Scriptural Roots of Christian Spirituality

All Christian spiritual traditions are rooted in the Scriptures. Behind the Christian Scriptures (the New Testament) lie the Jewish Scriptures (which Christians refer to as the Old Testament). Of course, Jesus of Nazareth and his first disciples were Jews, and the Christian Scriptures refer to the Jewish Scriptures in many different ways. In themselves, the Jewish Scriptures also play a significant role in the development of Christian spirituality across two thousand years, whether we think of the use of the Psalms or the Song of Solomon in mystical-contemplative literature and the powerful role of the book of Exodus in recent liberation spiritualities.

A fundamental scriptural image in Christian spirituality is discipleship. Indeed, the concept of discipleship was central to the pursuit of a Christian spiritual life. Christian spirituality is reducible neither to devotional practices nor an abstract theoretical framework.

---

[7] For more details on the history of the term *spirituality* and of its equivalents in the history of Christian spirituality, see Philip Sheldrake, *Spirituality and History: Questions of Interpretation and Method*, rev. ed. (Maryknoll, NY: Orbis Books, 1998), chapter 2, "What is Spirituality?"

Spirituality is a complete way of life. The concept of discipleship has two related dimensions. First, there is a call to conversion in response to the kingdom of God. "The time is fulfilled, and the kingdom of God has come near; repent, and believe in the good news" (Mark 1:15). The second dimension of following the way of Jesus is both to adopt a way of life and to continue the work of building God's kingdom. The first disciples were fishermen, and so the image of fishing plays a role. "And Jesus said to them, 'Follow me and I will make you fish for people' " (Mark 1:17). The same dual call to conversion and mission is present in the Gospel of Matthew (4:17, 19) and is also implicit in the Gospels of Luke and John.

Discipleship involves several elements. First, it is a response to a personal and collective call. Second, the title of disciple does not imply some kind of religious or moral perfection. After all, Jesus calls tax collectors and sinners (Matt 9:9) as well as all kinds of socially unacceptable people (Mark 2:15-17). Unusually for the time, women were also part of Jesus' immediate circle of followers (Luke 8:1-3). Third, the call to discipleship implies a radical break with the past that involves leaving everything that is familiar (see, for example, Luke 5:11 and 14:26; Mark 2:24 and 10:21) for the sake of the Gospel. The price of this radical change and transformation is sometimes characterized as taking up our cross or losing our life in order to truly find it (for example, Matt 10:38-39). Finally, discipleship implies sharing in the work of Jesus to bring God's kingdom into existence. For example, the great missionary discourse in the Gospel of Matthew, chapter 10, lists the work of the disciple as proclaiming the Good News, curing the sick, raising the dead, cleansing lepers, and casting out demons. To share in Jesus' work and life also involves the notion of radical service to other people (in Greek, *diakonia*), as in the Gospel of Mark 9:35, or of giving up one's life out of love (John 15:12-13).

In early Christian communities, discipleship moves strongly in two related directions. First, the disciple is not simply someone who follows the *teachings* of Jesus or who imitates the pattern of Jesus' life. The disciple is also to be profoundly *united* to Christ and, through this union, to share in Christ's own relationship with God the Father.[8]

---

[8] For a more extensive exploration of spirituality in relation to the New Testament, see Philip Sheldrake, *Spirituality: A Brief History*, 2nd ed. (Oxford: Wiley-Blackwell, 2013), chapter 2, 24–30.

Spirituality and History

The variety of spiritual traditions throughout history highlights a key characteristic of Christian spirituality—that it is inherently contextual. This is because Christianity as a whole is explicitly a historical religion. At its heart is the central doctrine of incarnation. This affirms that God embraced human existence in the person of Jesus of Nazareth at a particular moment in history. This explicitly links divine revelation and redemption to the processes of human history. In the words of the eminent British theologian and former archbishop of Canterbury, Rowan Williams, "By affirming that all 'meaning,' every assertion about the significance of life and reality, must be judged by reference to a brief succession of contingent events in Palestine, Christianity—almost without realising it—closed off the path to 'timeless truth.'"[9] Christian spirituality thereby affirms that the ambiguities and complexities of history are the essential context for spiritual transformation.

In thinking about the relationship between spirituality and history, a fundamental question is how we view the importance of history in itself. Contemporary Western cultures sometimes appear to be weary of the notion of being involved in a stream of tradition across time. "History" too often signifies merely the past—something interesting and perhaps romantic, but not vital for our future. "Tradition" is perceived by many people as a conservative force from which we need to break free. Consumer culture encourages a desire for immediacy. This also tends to produce a memory-less culture. During the twentieth century a further powerful factor was that the belief in history as a progressive force largely died out in the face of two world wars, mid-century totalitarianism, and the horrors of the Holocaust and Hiroshima.

However, despite some people's doubts, historical awareness is a human necessity. It reminds us that all our values, including spiritual ones, are unavoidably embedded in social and historical contexts. Attention to the complexities of history has been a major development in the study of Christian spirituality in recent decades. Following

---

[9] Rowan Williams, *The Wound of Knowledge* (London: Darton, Longman & Todd 1990), 1.

Williams's comment cited above, spiritual traditions do not exist on some detached plane above and beyond history. The origins and development of all spiritual traditions reflect the circumstances of time and place as well as the attitudes of the people involved. Consequently, spiritual traditions embody values that are historically shaped and conditioned. To take one example, as we shall see in the next chapter, the origins of early Christian ascetical movements, notably monasticism, involved a number of critical political, social, and economic factors in the fourth-century Roman Empire rather than resulting merely from abstract theological and spiritual principles in isolation.

To emphasize historical context and historical factors does not imply that spiritual traditions and classic texts have no value beyond their original time and place. However, it does mean that to appreciate their riches, we must take their historical context seriously. Context is not a "something" that may be added to or subtracted from spiritual experiences or traditions but is the very element within which these find expression.[10] This contradicts an older conception of Christian spirituality as a stream of enduring truth in which the same theories or images are simply repeated in different guises.

Periods and Traditions

This book seeks to present my choice of five types of Christian spirituality, as I shall outline in a moment. However, apart from the concept of types of spirituality, two of the most common organizing frameworks in histories of Christian spirituality are "periods" and "traditions." Because neither of these is straightforward, I will now offer a brief comment.

The concept of periods implies an essentially chronological approach to history.[11] However, choosing particular time boundaries to divide up a history of Christian spirituality is not a simple matter but involves choices and assumptions. For example, in writing a section about "spiritualities of the Reformation" how do we date "the

---

[10] See Sheldrake, *Spirituality and History*, 58, 84–86, 167–68; also Michel de Certeau, "Culture and Spiritual Experience," *Concilium* 19 (1966): 3–31.

[11] Sheldrake, *Spirituality and History*, chapter 4.

Reformation"? Do we emphasize continuities with the Middle Ages, or do we portray a complete rupture? More generally, do we take a short view of history or the long view in relation to whatever are considered to be the "main events"? Sometimes our choice of dates for a spiritual movement or tradition also depends on whether or not we give exclusive attention to "official" history related to religious authorities rather than to grassroots experience. Equally important is the question of our geographical focus.

Another frequently used framework for histories of Christian spirituality is the concept of traditions. There has been some debate about whether Christian spirituality should be treated as a single reality or as a plurality of different traditions.[12] In fact, the focus on unity or plurality is a matter of viewpoint. On the one hand, all Christian spiritual traditions take the life and teachings of Jesus Christ as their fundamental starting point. In that sense, there is unity. On the other hand, different traditions emerge precisely when people seek to respond to the Gospel in the context of their own time and place. In that sense, Christian spirituality is intrinsically plural.

As a fundamental point, a "spiritual tradition" implies a great deal more than the practice of a single exercise of piety or devotion. Rather, it embodies some significant spiritual wisdom (usually expressed in key texts or in ways of life) that distinguishes it from other traditions. However, an implicit question is whether and how it is possible to say when a particular form of spirituality has clearly become a *tradition* in the fullest sense rather than simply a passing trend. This is not straightforward, particularly when a form of spirituality has emerged relatively recently. Some broad guidelines may be helpful. First, is there evidence of the existence of a generation or more of practitioners who had no firsthand experience of the founder(s) or origins of the particular tradition? Second, has the tradition established certain classic texts, documentation, or structures for the transmission of that tradition? Third, has the spiritual wisdom embodied in a community of practitioners shown itself clearly capable of moving beyond its time and place of origin?

It is important to note that the notion of how a "spiritual tradition" is interpreted and handed on has undergone further development in

---

[12] For a summary of this debate, see Sheldrake, *Spirituality and History*, 196–98.

the relatively recent movement known as "traditioning" developed by Christians of Central and Latin American origin. This relatively new approach confronts the complex issue of reappropriating, or even sometimes resisting, historic spiritual traditions. The fundamental question is how Christian spirituality transmits itself and how it is received across cultural boundaries. There is clearly a question of content—that is, something quite specific is handed on or "traditioned." However, traditioning focuses far more on the *process* of transmission. There are four key elements. First, we must attend to the way in which classic traditions born in one culture (for example, Western Europe) now enter a new cultural context. Second, we must value what is termed *lo cotidiano*—the everyday. This is the authentic reappropriation of spiritual traditions in relation to the questions and situations of daily life in a local community. Third, there is a need to give a higher valuation to popular religion rather than simply to sophisticated structures and texts. Approaches to Christian spirituality have often been limited by predominently intellectual presuppositions. We need to embrace expressions of the sacred in rituals, devotions, shrines, and pilgrimage, for example. Finally, traditioning invites us to consider how the transmission of spiritual traditions depends not simply on religious authorities or on technical "experts" but also on a consensus among the broader Christian community, who in reality are the "ordinary" transmitters of any tradition.[13]

Christian Spirituality as Transformation and Mission

It is important to note briefly the fundamental characteristics of all historic forms of Christian spirituality. As already described, we need to begin with the Scriptures.

With this basis, it is possible to say that, taken as a whole, the foundations of Christian spirituality involve a way of transformation toward the fullness of life in God and, at the same time, a way of mission through following the pattern of Jesus Christ while being empowered by God's indwelling Spirit. Transformation and mission

---

[13] On the principles of "traditioning," see Orlando O. Espin and Gary Macy, eds., *Futuring our Past: Explorations in the Theology of Tradition* (Maryknoll, NY: Orbis Books, 2006).

are the key ideas for understanding all Christian spirituality. Every Christian spiritual tradition is an articulation in specific time-place contexts of the New Testament model of following Jesus faithfully. Jesus' life and teachings are the measure of all authentic forms of Christian spirituality. Yet, at the same time, the particularity of the life and context of Jesus Christ permits the equally particular nature of all subsequent discipleship.[14]

The history of Christian spirituality is a rich and varied expression of how the call to transformation and mission is to be understood. All classic spiritual traditions explicitly or implicitly address certain questions. First, what needs to be transformed, or what are we to be transformed from and why? In other words, spiritual traditions offer a perspective on the nature of, and remedies for, human disorder. Second, what factors stand in the way of our transformation? These factors are often described theologically, although nowadays we also take note of psychological or social factors. Third, where does transformation take place? Is the context for transformation normal, everyday life, or is it set apart in some kind of special place (for example, the desert or the monastery)? Fourth, how does transformation take place? This often involves some theory of spiritual growth as well as wisdom about lifestyles or spiritual practices that aid transformation. Finally, what is the purpose of transformation, and where does it lead?

Different spiritual traditions offer varied theories of spiritual transformation and wisdom about the lifestyles or spiritual practices that assist this. A common image is that of a pilgrimage or journey with various stages or dimensions. This has been expressed in different times and places through themes such as *theosis* (or deification), ascent (up mountains or ladders), or the *triplex via* (or threefold path). In broader terms, the theme of the Christian life as a pilgrimage has been richly expressed in spiritual literature ranging from Augustine's *City of God* to John Bunyan's seventeenth-century *Pilgrim's Progress* and onward to the anonymous nineteenth-century Russian work on

---

[14] For a more developed treatment of this idea, see the essay by the great French Jesuit scholar of spirituality Michel de Certeau, "How is Christianity Thinkable Today?," translated in *The Postmodern God*, ed. Graham Ward (Oxford: Blackwell, 1997).

the spirituality of the Jesus Prayer, *The Way of the Pilgrim*. The metaphor of a journey expresses the radically dynamic nature of the Christian spiritual life. Sometimes two rather static concepts, "perfection" and "union," have been used to express the end point of the spiritual journey. However, the end in view is ultimately a more mysterious and dynamic entering into fullness of life in God.

The theology of the early church gradually developed a theory of stages in the spiritual life. The Alexandrian theologian Origen (ca. 185–255) explained the contemplative life in neoplatonic terms as three ascending stages associated with beginners (*praxis*), proficients (*theōria*), and the perfect (*theologia*), moving away from our material existence and toward a greater light.[15] The goal of the journey was a recovery of the original created likeness of God in the soul. In the following century, the Cappadocian theologian Gregory of Nyssa (ca. 335–395), especially in his *Life of Moses*, also described the contemplative journey in terms of the stages of ascent. However, in this case it was toward darkness rather than light. Gregory used the metaphor of Moses on Mount Sinai entering into ever-deeper clouds of darkness in his encounter with God.[16] Because Gregory of Nyssa has an apophatic (that is, imageless) understanding of the climax of the spiritual journey as a deep darkness in which God is experienced but never definitively *known*, there is an open-ended quality to his teachings about spiritual transformation.

Origen's and Gregory's expositions of the spiritual journey (allied with the mystical theology of the sixth-century anonymous monk commonly known as Pseudo-Dionysius) had a considerable influence in both Eastern and Western Christianity. During the Middle Ages, the Western approach to the spiritual journey developed strongly in the direction of what became known as the "three ways" or *triplex via* (purgative, illuminative, and unitive ways). These were often described in terms of consecutive stages, although in practice they are more properly intersecting dimensions of transformation. Subsequent spiritual literature also employs metaphors for the spiritual

[15] See "The Prologue to the Commentary on the Song of Songs" in *Origen*, ed. and trans. Rowan A. Greer, Classics of Western Spirituality (Mahwah, NJ: Paulist Press, 1979).

[16] See Everett Ferguson and Abraham J. Malherbe, trans. and eds., *Gregory of Nyssa: The Life of Moses*, Classics of Western Spirituality (Mahwah, NJ: Paulist Press, 1978).

journey. Often this is the classic theme of ascent, whether of ladders—for example, Walter Hilton's fourteenth-century *Ladder* or *Scale* (from the Latin *scala*, "stairs") *of Perfection*—or of mountains, such as the sixteenth-century *Ascent of Mount Carmel* by John of the Cross.

The dominant Western monastic rule, the sixth-century Rule of St. Benedict, also described the spiritual journey in terms of a ladder. The twelve degrees of humility in its chapter 7 are "a ladder of our ascending actions." This is developed further in monastic commentaries such as that by the twelfth-century Cistercian Bernard of Clairvaux, *Steps of Humility and Pride*. Another influential monastic description of the spiritual journey was the twelfth-century *Ladder of Monks*, by Guigo II, a Carthusian. However, this referred to the ancient contemplative practice of reading Scripture known as *lectio divina*, now structured more systematically as four stages known as *lectio, meditatio, oratio,* and *contemplatio*.[17]

The classic metaphor of ascent, or the notion of stages, retains a certain contemporary value by emphasizing a continuous journey rather than a succession of disconnected experiences. However, historically the notion of stages also suggested a growing separation of oneself from the material world in order to lead a truly spiritual life. This is problematic. There are also some more general questions about the notion of successive stages. First, what are represented as distinct stages (purgation/repentance, illumination/enlargement of vision, and union with God) are in practice likely to be present in different ways at all points of the spiritual journey. Second, union with God should not be understood merely as yet another stage beyond previous stages to be achieved through contemplative practice. In one sense, our fundamental union with God in our creation is a precondition of the spiritual journey as a whole. Equally, the notion of a final union beyond time is a mysterious gift that defies definition. Third, the notion of distinct stages can support a questionable hierarchy of spiritual values and lifestyles in which the contemplative way is seen as distinct from, and superior to, the way of everyday life and action.

---

[17] See Edmund Colledge and James Walsh, trans., *Guigo II: Ladder of Monks and Twelve Meditations* (Collegeville, MN: Cistercian Publications, 1981).

While classic approaches to the spiritual journey in Christian spirituality continue to offer valuable wisdom for our own times, a contemporary perspective suggests that their somewhat individualistic approach should nowadays be complemented by the renewed biblical emphasis on a collective understanding of Christian discipleship. For example, Vatican II clearly emphasized that it is the Christian community as a whole that is a pilgrim people "led by the Holy Spirit in their journey to the kingdom of their Father" (*Gaudium et Spes* 1). As we shall see in chapter 6, this recovery of a more collective understanding of the spiritual journey also underpinned the theme of solidarity with others expressed by liberation theology and spirituality as they emerged in Latin America in the late 1960s. This included the use of the Old Testament image of the Exodus, a desert journey in which God leads the oppressed peoples from a state of slavery to the possession of a land of their own—for example, in the work of Gustavo Gutiérrez.[18]

Christian Spirituality and Theology

Because contemporary understandings of the word *spirituality* tend to distinguish it from religion, an intimate connection between spirituality and theology seems to be counterintuitive. However, within the context of a specifically Christian approach to spirituality, this connection is unavoidable. In discussions about how theology and Christian spirituality relate to each other, there have been several schools of thought among contemporary scholars. The first approach suggests that spirituality is an autonomous discipline, distinct from theology while related to it. The second approach prefers to treat Christian spirituality as a part of theology, albeit one that has a dis-

---

[18] For example, Gustavo Gutiérrez, *We Drink from Our Own Wells: The Spiritual Journey of a People* (Maryknoll, NY: Orbis Books, 1984). For discussions of the different approaches to the spiritual journey in Christian spirituality, see, for example, Lawrence S. Cunningham and Keith J. Egan, *Christian Spirituality: Themes from the Tradition* (Mahwah, NJ: Paulist Press, 1996); Andrew Louth, *The Origins of the Christian Mystical Tradition: From Plato to Denys* (Oxford: Clarendon Press, 1981); and Margaret R. Miles, *Practicing Christianity: Critical Perspectives for an Embodied Spirituality* (New York: Crossroad, 1988).

tinctive identity. Finally, some scholars have attempted to bridge the divide between these two approaches.

A significant representative of the first position is the New Testament scholar Sandra Schneiders, who is also one of the most influential figures in the contemporary development of Christian spirituality as an academic field.[19] Schneiders believes that spirituality and theology are close partners that mutually assist, but are autonomous from, each other. In reaction to older approaches to spiritual theology, Schneiders is concerned that contemporary Christian spirituality should not be seen as a subdivision of one of the traditional theological disciplines, such as systematic theology, historical theology, or moral theology. She affirms that theology should not be seen as a straightforward container for spirituality because the field is inherently interdisciplinary. Even in a Christian context, spirituality should no longer be seen as merely the practical expression of Christian doctrines.

The second viewpoint is represented by the eminent American historian of mysticism, Bernard McGinn. McGinn believes that spirituality has a priority in its partnership with theology, and so he rejects the old-fashioned view that spirituality was derived in some simple way from dogmatic theology. Nevertheless, McGinn is concerned that the nature of religious experience and the spiritual journey should properly be a concern of theology as a whole. He is therefore nervous about separating spirituality from theology in any way. Consequently, McGinn believes that spirituality is best taught within a combination of theological disciplines: systematics, historical theology, ethics, and the history of Christianity. Following Hans Urs von Balthasar, McGinn believes that the particularity of Christian spiritual experience demands that theology be the primary criterion of its interpretation.[20]

---

[19] See, for example, Sandra Schneiders, "Approaches to the Study of Christian Spirituality," in *The Blackwell Companion to Christian Spirituality*, ed. Arthur Holder (Malden, MA: Blackwell, 2005), 15–33; also Sandra Schneiders, "The Study of Christian Spirituality: Contours and Dynamics of a Discipline," in *Minding the Spirit: The Study of Christian Spirituality*, ed. Elizabeth Dreyer and Mark Burrows (Baltimore, MD: Johns Hopkins University Press, 2005), 5–24.

[20] Bernard McGinn, "The Letter and the Spirit: Spirituality as an Academic Discipline," in *Minding the Spirit*, ed. Dreyer and Burrows, 25–41.

My own view, shared by a number of other theologians with an interest in Christian spirituality, is that we do not need to make a sharp contrast between these two positions. Broadly speaking, I would argue that while a relationship between Christian spirituality and theology is central, nevertheless Christian spirituality has a distinct identity. In this context, the important word is *distinct* rather than *autonomous*. In different ways, these theologians suggest that, within the overall theological enterprise, there is the need for a "turn to spirituality." Theology needs to realize more effectively its own essentially spiritual core. Theology must also seek to enter into dialogue with Christian spirituality in a way that is radically different from the more familiar conversations with philosophy, history, and other intellectual disciplines. This dialogue with spirituality necessarily involves allowing theological discourse to be questioned by the deeper insight that the reality of God is beyond the "God" of definitions and theological systems. The indefinable reality of God is more likely to be encountered by the ways of "knowing" evoked by mystical texts. From the perspective of conceptual thought, these are also radical ways of "unknowing" or negation.[21]

Theology Evaluating Spirituality

How do spirituality and theology relate to each other? To take one example, the writings of Chicago theologian David Tracy offer useful theological ways of evaluating spirituality. He suggests that one criterion is whether a spiritual tradition meets the basic demands of contemporary understanding and wisdom. Tracy refers to this approach as "criteria of adequacy." Beyond this fundamental level, other ways of evaluating spirituality relate to specifically Christian understandings of existence. Tracy refers to this as "criteria of appropriateness."

The application of criteria of adequacy is not a reduction of Christian theology and spirituality to purely secular norms. In terms of

---

[21] For an overview of the debates about the relationship of spirituality and theology, see Philip Sheldrake, *Spirituality and Theology: Christian Living and the Doctrine of God* (Maryknoll, NY: Orbis Books, 1999), chapter 3, "Partners in Conversation"; also *Explorations in Spirituality: History, Theology and Social Practice* (Mahwah, NJ: Paulist Books, 2010), chapter 3, "Spirituality and Theology: Belief and Practice."

spirituality, it implies that it cannot ignore generally accepted developments in human knowledge. Nor can spirituality ignore the ways in which previously overconfident views of human progress have been undermined by the painful historical events of the twentieth century. To put it simply, we have to take into account the new worlds of understanding and interpretation developed by evolutionary theory, psychology, and the social and political sciences, and more recently by cosmology and quantum theory. Equally, Christian spirituality can never be the same after the Holocaust and Hiroshima.

In Tracy's terms, there are three broad criteria of adequacy. First, every religious interpretation of experience needs to be adequately rooted in common human experience. Second, a religious understanding of experience should be intellectually coherent. Third, all authentic spiritual traditions need to throw light on the underlying conditions of life, not least to say whether our human confidence in life is actually worthwhile.

In terms of criteria of appropriateness, overall any tradition or type of spirituality should point us toward a God worthy of loving commitment. More broadly, an adequate understanding of Christian spirituality must relate in some way to classic Christian beliefs. Far from being irrelevant, the God language of Trinity and incarnation implicitly critiques any spirituality that is preoccupied only with self-realization or achieving happiness. Allowing for legitimate diversity and differences of emphasis, traditions of spirituality should embrace the whole Gospel rather than be one sided or unbalanced. For example, what models of holiness are suggested? Is the view of human nature dualistic, with a low theology of embodiment? Is there a balanced and healthy approach to sexuality? Understandings of prayer and contemplation are central in Christian spirituality. Does a particular spiritual tradition view relate prayer to a wider approach to human and Christian life? Is there a balance between contemplation and action? Of its nature, Christian spirituality cannot avoid the question of tradition. What is the role of Scripture and tradition? Finally, an important question is whether a particular spiritual tradition has a developed eschatology and specifically one that encourages an appropriate balance between "the now" and "the not yet."[22]

---

[22] See David Tracy, *Blessed Rage for Order* (New York: Seabury Press, 1975), 64–79.

Spirituality Evaluating Theology

Conversely, spiritual traditions offer criteria to judge the adequacy of theology. A fundamental question concerns whether theology offers not simply an attempt at intellectual coherence in relation to understandings of God or human identity but also a way of knowledge that relates to the practice of a Christian life and enhances a sense of the presence of God. The British Orthodox theologian Andrew Louth suggests that "Spirituality [is] that which keeps theology to its proper vocation, that which prevents theology from evading its own real object. Spirituality does not really answer the question, Who is God? but it preserves the orientation, the perspective, within which this question remains a question that is being evaded or chided."[23] To put it another way, spirituality reminds us that to "do" theology is fundamentally practical. In the context of academic study, this view implies that what is sometimes called "practical theology" should not be an optional extra within the theological core curriculum. However, the place of practice in theology means something more. Theology is not merely concerned with content or resources. To do theology means becoming a theological person in the deepest spiritual sense, not merely using theological tools.

Being a theological person implies more than intellectual exploration. The ancient meaning of *theologia* is a much broader concept than theology as a modern academic field. It inevitably involves what Eastern Orthodox Christianity has called *theoria*. At first sight, this word is misleading to Western eyes. It is more accurately translated as "contemplation" rather than "theory." The committed believer is one who lives theology rather than does it as an activity detached from who she or he is. Sadly, there is still a tendency in Western thought to think and act as if *knowledge* means something purely objective and rational. But theology in its richest sense is essentially performative as well as informative; it is concerned with action as well as ideas. Consequently, the title *theologian* does not imply someone who provides specialized analysis and information while standing at a personal distance from the object of reflection. "Being a theolo-

---

[23] Andrew Louth, *Theology and Spirituality,* Fairacres Publications 55 (Oxford: SLG Press, 1978), 4.

gian" involves a quality of presence to the reality we reflect upon as much as a concern for the techniques of a specific discipline.

The ancient meaning of a theologian as a person who sees and experiences the content of theological reflection connects well with contemporary understandings of the self-implicating nature of study. Theology and spirituality in their fullest sense are self-implicating. This does not imply anti-intellectualism. There needs to be a critical approach to both theology and spirituality, but critical analysis is the servant of good theology and not, surely, what theologians do or live theology for. In both theology and spirituality, a kind of transformation is implied by the search for knowledge.

Spirituality also offers a vital critique of any attempt by theology to launch itself into some stratosphere of timeless truth, abstract distinction, or ungrounded definition. The way that spirituality "speaks" of God is radically different from the approach of old-fashioned systematic or fundamental theology. If theology turns to spirituality and allows its systems to be questioned, it will find that spirituality recognizes that what is implied by the word *God* cannot ultimately be spoken completely.

One of the most fundamental aspects of the Christian doctrine of God is that the human quest for God demands a paradox of both knowing and not knowing. This has particular force in the context of a conversation between spirituality and theology. The words *cataphatic* and *apophatic* have often been used to describe the two sides of human relations with God. The cataphatic element emphasizes the way of imaging. It is a positive theology or a theology of affirmation based on a high doctrine of creation and human life as contexts for God's self-revelation. The apophatic element, in contrast, emphasizes "not knowing," silence, darkness, and the absence of imagery. It is a negative theology or a theology of denial. A sixth-century pseudonymous Eastern writer known as Dionysius (or Denis) the Areopagite was one of the most influential exponents of the concepts of apophatic and cataphatic theologies. He had a major impact on Western theology and mysticism. In Dionysius's approach to God, knowing and unknowing are mutually related rather than mutually exclusive.

It is worth noting that a number of modern theologians have been fascinated by the theological possibilities of mystical writings. One example is David Tracy, already mentioned. He suggests that in our present era "we may now learn to drop earlier dismissals of 'mysticism' and allow its uncanny negations to release us."[24] This reflects Tracy's own journey toward a belief that the apophatic language of the mystics is where theologians must turn in our present times. "As critical and speculative philosophical theologians and artists learn to let go into the sensed reality of some event of manifestation, some experience of releasement and primal thinking, a sense of the reality of mystical experience can begin to show itself in itself. Even those with no explicit mystical experience, like myself, sense that thinking can become thanking, that silence does become, even for an Aquinas when he would 'write no more', the final form of speech possible to any authentic speaker."[25] In the West we have inherited a tendency to believe that knowledge means only abstract intelligence and objective analysis. The problem with theological knowledge is that while we may be impelled to speak of God, we cannot in the end speak definitively about God in the sense of capturing the divine. The problem with a purely intellectual search for God is that it necessarily regards what is sought as an object or an objective that can be reached. Insofar as we can, in Christian terms, speak of the human search for God, it will be a search that continually fails to capture or find God in any definitive sense.

Characteristics of Christian Spirituality

It is now possible and important to outline certain fundamental characteristics of all forms of Christian spirituality. For example, Christian spirituality is intimately related to a specific understanding of God and of God's relationship with the world and with human beings. God is described as Trinity, a dynamic interrelationship of "persons in communion." This complex understanding of God clearly underlines that God's existence is totally "other," beyond the capacity of human language to define and beyond human powers to control. However, this understanding of God also embraces a belief that the

---

[24] David Tracy, *The Analogical Imagination: Christian Theology and the Culture of Pluralism* (New York: Crossroad, 1991), 360.

[25] Tracy, *Analogical Imagination*, 385.

divine life overflows into an eternal dynamism of creativity. Christian spirituality is creation-centered in the sense that it understands that all material reality is the gift of, and a reflection of, a loving God.

Closely related to this is the doctrine of God's "incarnation." God's engagement with humanity is expressed particularly by taking on embodied, historic existence in the person of Jesus of Nazareth, who came to be known as the Christ or the Anointed One. This makes all Christian spiritual traditions Christ-centered in different ways. Another corollary, as we have already seen, is that Christian spirituality, like Christianity itself, necessarily takes history seriously. Also, as already noted, the fundamental framework for understanding the Christian life is discipleship, which implies both *metanoia*, or "conversion," and also following a way of life in the pattern of Jesus Christ as a prolongation of his mission.

As a consequence, Christian spirituality, when it is true to its foundations, has a fundamentally positive view of the material world and of the human body. Such an approach to spirituality may be said to be "sacramental" in the sense that material reality (including our embodied selves and everyday experience and action) is understood to be the medium for God's self-revelation and for human encounters with the sacred. This sacramentality is expressed particularly in the rituals of Christian sacraments, notably the Eucharist. However, despite this positive view of the material world as a revelation of the sacred, Christian understandings of God's creativity and relationship to humanity are not naively optimistic. Christian spirituality in all its forms recognizes disorder and sin in the world. Consequently, God's relationship to humanity is also seen as redemptive. That is, in the person of Jesus, God is believed to confront human disorder with a call to repentance and at the same time with the promise of ultimate restoration.

Importantly, as already noted, Christian discipleship is not individualistic. It is essentially communal, within the community of believers, sustained by a common life and shared rituals, and expressed ideally in mutual love and acceptance. In fact, the heart of Christian spirituality is precisely a way of life rather than an abstract code of beliefs. At the center of Christian understandings of spiritual transformation is the notion of God's abiding presence in the Christian community and also God's indwelling in every person as Spirit. The

Spirit of God empowers, guides, and inspires the journey of the Christian community and of each person toward an ultimate union with the divine in eternal life.

Finally, while Christian spirituality affirms the value of creation and of history, the journey of spiritual transformation leads beyond history into an eschatological future. In that sense, authentic spirituality responds to everyday life yet, at the same time, subverts our tendency to settle on what we can see, grasp, and control as the only measure of our existence.

Conclusion

Unfortunately, in the context of a growing interest in "spirituality," not least in Western countries, Christianity has not always helped its own cause. In the popular mind, Christianity is too often equated with institutional structures, with dogma, moralism, authoritarianism, and an excessive concern for money, systems, and buildings. The fact that Christianity is fundamentally based on a spiritual vision is lost. Yet, as this book aims to show, throughout history Christianity has given rise to a wide range of spiritual traditions that have the potential to offer spiritual wisdom, spiritual practices, and a path for the spiritual journey to the wider world.

CHAPTER TWO

The Way of Discipline

The first type of Christian spirituality that I wish to focus on is what I call the Way of Discipline. This approach is closely associated with the notion of asceticism as an important spiritual value. Unfortunately, these days, the word *asceticism* often provokes negative reactions. This is because it has become associated with images of self-punishment related to a fundamentally negative, sin-ridden, understanding of human identity. The word can sound masochistic and unhealthy. Therefore, a critical question is whether the notion of discipline, including asceticism, can be redeemed in relation to contemporary approaches to spirituality.

The modern word *asceticism* derives from the ancient Greek word *askēsis*. This, broadly speaking, means "training" or "discipline" and probably originates in the world of athletics. It implies an ordered and focused lifestyle. Overall, properly understood, asceticism suggests a rejection of the idea that human fulfillment can be achieved through seeking material success or by consumption. Asceticism tends to prescribe the practice of abstention from material pleasure as the measure of a satisfactory life and as the pathway to perfection.

Clearly, this type of spirituality may be practiced through the medium of a focused and disciplined everyday life. However, historically, spiritual traditions under the heading of the Way of Discipline often recommended withdrawing to special places to enable the process of spiritual transformation. Examples include living within the austerity and isolation of certain kinds of natural landscape, such as the desert or mountains, or the structured life of a monastery or periodic withdrawal to a retreat house. Overall, this type of spirituality focuses on a disciplined rather than a fragmented or dissipated life. The end product may be summarized as freedom from material preoccupations and deepened moral behavior.

In Christianity, as in several other world religions, forms of monastic life became iconic examples in relation to this type of spirituality. Importantly, in Christian monasticism and other "disciplined" forms of spirituality, the true purpose of discipline or asceticism is not to punish the body or to reject everyday life as of little value. Rather, the Way of Discipline is intended to bring about liberation from whatever impedes our spiritual progress, such as unbalanced dependencies, not least on material possessions—or "freedom from disordered attachments" in the language of Ignatius of Loyola's *Spiritual Exercises*.

The Birth of Christian Monasticism

In early Christianity, up to the early fourth century CE, *askēsis* or disciplined training focused on ensuring steadfastness in the face of a threat of persecution and martyrdom. However, the period from the fourth century onward saw a major consolidation of Christianity because of complex changes in the surrounding political and cultural landscape. First of all, Christianity emerged into the public mainstream as a result of the Emperor Constantine's edict of toleration (313 CE) and subsequently became the official religion of the Roman Empire.

Inevitably, this led to readjustments in self-understanding and in spiritual values. The ascetical movements that gave birth to monasticism were in many ways a countercultural reaction to the Christian church joining the political and social establishment and becoming an increasingly dominant group in Roman society.

Over the next few centuries, the history of Christian spirituality in both East and West was in many ways dominated by ascetical-monastic spirituality—an example of the type I refer to as the Way of Discipline. There gradually developed a sense that lifelong "discipline" should be valued more highly than momentary steadfastness in the face of possible martyrdom. The monk inherited the role of the martyr, literally bearing witness to the action of God and to the teachings of the Christian Scriptures, as well as being an intercessor on behalf of the community and giving unwavering attention to God by living a life freed from material distractions. This process was sometimes actually referred to as "white martyrdom."

A Movement to the Margins

Christian monasticism is essentially a movement to the margins. The wilderness (desert, mountain, forest, or sea) has exercised a peculiar fascination throughout Christian history. One of the fundamental features of Christian monasticism is that it demands withdrawal. The theme of the desert is common to many monastic texts. There was a special association between deep spiritual experience and the desert—whether understood literally or figuratively. Why were physical deserts and other wilderness territories chosen for monastic groups? Wilderness may be both a renewal of paradise, where people lived in harmony with wild animals, and at the same time a place of trial where ascetics struggled with inner and outer demons. Wilderness is essentially frontier territory, and living there symbolizes a state of liminality—existing between two worlds, the material and the spiritual.

The desert was originally associated with a spiritual journey through death to rebirth. It was to be a metaphorical tomb before the tomb. It is recorded in Athanasius's *Life of Anthony* that Antony of Egypt began his hermit life in the desert by literally sleeping in an ancient tomb. What more powerful symbol could there be of a loss of conventional human needs and priorities?[1] However, the underlying values of early desert monasticism were that through struggle, physical deprivation, and submission, both to a spiritual guide and to the challenges of an empty landscape, the monk is enabled to enter into a new life in Christ.

To move to the desert was, both literally and metaphorically, a journey toward a holy place and also away from the "world" or the human city as a place of sin. To be perfected spiritually demanded a

---

[1] Robert C. Gregg, ed., *Athanasius: The Life of Anthony* (Mahwah, NJ: Paulist Press, 1980), paragraph 8, 37–39.

physical displacement. The early ascetics in Syria, Palestine, and Egypt, from the late third century CE onward, deliberately sought out the empty spaces of the wilderness as the context for inner spiritual combat. One aspect of this seems to have been a desire to be freed from conventional social identity and normal social ties. Thus, monastic disengagement was from the start a social statement as well as a spiritual one.[2]

The Wisdom of the Desert

Organized monasticism first emerged in Egypt during the early fourth century CE. The movement remained essentially a lay one. Egyptian monasticism developed in three broad forms associated with geographical locations. By 400 CE it numbered many thousands of women and men. The first, and earliest, form was the hermit life of which Antony of Egypt was the archetype. This flourished especially in what was called Lower Egypt to the immediate south of the Nile Delta. Antony withdrew into solitude circa 269 CE and gradually went further into the desert wilderness. Yet he attracted many disciples seeking guidance. The notion of total solitude needs some modification, as two hermits sometimes lived together and disciples stayed in close proximity to their spiritual guides. The second form consisted of small groups of ascetics who lived to the West of the Nile Delta. These groups gathered around a spiritual father (*abba*) or mother (*amma*) in "villages," known as a *lavra* or *skete*. The most famous settlements were at Nitria and Scetis, near Alexandria, which became important meeting places of desert and urban worlds. A more educated monasticism evolved around theologically sophisticated figures such as Evagrius (345–399 CE). The third form of monasticism was in Upper (or southern) Egypt, close to the ancient city of Thebes. This form consisted of relatively ordered and large communities of men or women. The leading figure was Pachomius (290–347 CE), who founded the settlement of Tabennisis, which is conventionally described as the origin of structured monasticism.

---

[2] See Peter Brown, *The Making of Late Antiquity* (Cambridge, MA: Harvard University Press, 1993), chapter 4, "From the Heavens to the Desert: Anthony and Pachomius."

The principal sources for the spiritual wisdom of desert monasticism, apart from lives of the great founders (for example, Athanasius's *Life of Anthony*) were collections of sayings and anecdotes. These were initially passed on orally and later written down during the fifth century in texts known as the *Apophthegmata Patrum*. Two major collections were organized by subject matter (the Systematic Series) and under the names of the well-known teachers (the Alphabetical Collection).[3] These writings reflect a period of informality. Once large communities were founded, normative texts such as the Rule of Pachomius began to appear.[4]

The desert ascetics wished to live the life demanded of all Christians, but with particular intensity. They simply sought the way to salvation. "A brother asked a hermit, 'What must I do to be saved?' He took off his clothes, and put a girdle about his loins and stretched out his hands and said, 'Thus ought the monk to be: stripped naked of everything, and crucified by temptation and combat with the world.' "[5] This story illustrates two other key elements of desert spirituality that passed into later monastic traditions. The first theme is spiritual combat or warfare—battling with temptation or even literally with demons. So, for example, "They said of Sarah that for thirteen years she was fiercely attacked by the demon of lust. She never prayed that the battle would leave her, but she used to say only, 'Lord, give me strength.' "[6] Mature desert ascetics, such as Sarah, did not pray to be relieved from temptations. Indeed, sometimes they even asked their spiritual guide to pray that temptation continue because they believed that struggle in itself had a spiritual value. A second, related theme is asceticism. Understood properly, asceticism

[3] An excellent selection, translated and introduced by the scholar of early monasticism, Sister Benedicta Ward, contains examples from both collections. See Benedicta Ward, trans., *The Desert Fathers: Sayings of the Early Christian Monks* (London: Penguin Books, 2003).

[4] The most comprehensive recent study of desert monasticism is William Harmless, *Desert Christians: An Introduction to the Literature of Early Monasticism* (Oxford: Oxford University Press, 2004). One of the best studies of early desert spirituality is Douglas Burton-Christie, *The Word in the Desert* (Oxford: Oxford University Press, 1993). There is an excellent short summary of desert spirituality in Andrew Louth, *The Wilderness of God* (London: Darton, Longman & Todd, 1991), chapter 3.

[5] Ward, *The Desert Fathers*, 57, number 16.

[6] Ward, *The Desert Fathers*, 36, number 10.

does not imply an anti-body attitude but takes the body with great seriousness, as it is a vital element of spiritual progress that is simply in need of proper ordering. The goal of ascetical discipline was a properly directed life rather than a fragmented life.[7]

The greatest channels of spiritual wisdom were the hermit's cell and the spiritual guide. The action of staying in the cell, even when tempted, was a practical discipline and a spiritual symbol. Practically, the cell provided silence, solitude, and the absence of external distraction. This enabled the practice of continuous prayer. Symbolically, the simplicity of the cell represented a shedding of worldly possessions, and staying there faithfully represented the value of stability and endurance as the foundations for the spiritual journey. "In Scetis a brother went to Moses to ask for advice. He said to him, 'Go and sit in your cell, and your cell will teach you everything.'"[8] This quotation also expresses the strength of the relationship between ascetics and their spiritual guides.[9] In the hermit or *skete ways* of life, reliance on the spiritual father or mother was vital for practical advice about how to survive the rigors of desert life, how to avoid illusion, and how to become wise in the ways of the heart. People chose their spiritual guides because of their wisdom and experience. In general there were no lengthy conversations or detailed instructions. Rather, the practice was a few words and pithy sayings. At the heart of the relationship was obedience. This was a discipline that corrected any tendency to rely on one's own powers and also expressed receptivity to God. "A hermit said, 'Someone who hands over his soul in obedience to a spiritual guide has a greater reward than one who retires alone to a hermitage.'"[10]

The theme of obedience highlights two further central values of the desert tradition: humility and discernment. The cultivation of

---

[7] For a brief but first-rate summary of asceticism and the role of the body in the desert tradition, see Peter Brown, *The Body and Society: Men, Women and Sexual Renunciation in Early Christianity* (London: Faber & Faber, 1991), chapter 11.

[8] Ward, *The Desert Fathers*, 10, number 9.

[9] On spiritual guidance in the desert, see the classic study by Irénée Hausherr, *Spiritual Direction in the Early Christian East* (Kalamazoo, MI: Cistercian Publications, 1990). This edition includes an excellent summary of the tradition in the foreword by Kallistos Ware. See also Benedicta Ward, "Spiritual Direction in the Desert Fathers," in *The Way* 24/1 (January 1984): 61–70.

[10] Ward, *The Desert Fathers*, 147, number 19.

honesty and self-awareness—the real meaning of humility—was thought to be a critical means of spiritual progress. It was the greatest defense against spiritual pride, which was seen as the classic temptation of the hermit. Humility was often linked to a capacity to forgive others their faults.

> A hermit was asked, "What is humility?" He answered, "Humility is a great work and a work of God. The way of humility is to undertake bodily labour, and believe yourself a sinner, and make yourself the servant of all." A brother said, "What does that mean, to be the servant of all?" He answered, "To be the servant of all is not to look at the sins of others, always to look at your own sins, and to pray to God without ceasing."[11]

Discernment or spiritual wisdom ("discretion")—the capacity to judge well and to choose properly—was the most prized of the ascetic virtues. In the minds of desert ascetics, it was often associated with an ability to recognize the difference between the inspiration of God and the promptings of the demons. Discernment was a gift of God received through deep prayer and ascetic practice. It marked out the true ascetic from the spiritual gymnast who carried out prodigious acts of endurance in an unbalanced way. "A hermit was asked by a brother, 'How do I find God? With fasts, or labour, or vigils, or works of mercy?' He replied, 'You will find Him in all those, and also in discretion. I tell you, many have been very stern with their bodies, but have gained nothing by it because they did it without discretion. Even if our mouths stink from fasting, and we have learnt all the Scriptures, and memorized the whole Psalter, we may still lack what God wants, humility and love.'"[12] If God seeks humility, God also seeks charity. A lack of self-centeredness should overflow into care for others. The desert ascetics were very clear that their spiritual way was not one of self-preoccupation but rather of ever-greater sensitivity to those people who were in need, and of the freedom to respond. The scriptural injunction to love God and neighbor was always before their eyes. "A brother asked a hermit, 'Suppose there are two monks: one stays quietly in his cell, fasting for six days at a time, laying many

---

[11] Ibid., 167, number 82.
[12] Ibid., 111, number 94.

hardships on himself: and the other ministers to the sick. Which of them is more pleasing to God?' He replied, 'Even if the brother who fasts six days hung himself up by his nose, he wouldn't be the equal of him who ministers to the sick.'"[13]

In terms of spiritual practices, what was done should serve the fundamental values of the ascetical life: discipline, spiritual struggle, endurance, charity, and, above all, discernment. When we read the sayings and lives of the desert ascetics, silence and staying in one's cell played a central role. The practice of "unceasing prayer" might imply extended meditation or long vigils, or it might mean praying "in the heart" while doing other tasks, such as manual labor.

Indeed, apart from practical necessity, manual labor was also a spiritual discipline that countered the temptation to be idle. Fasting or a broader frugality underlined the value of bodily self-control. However, it is also striking in the desert sayings and stories that charity and hospitality had a high priority. An ascetic might put aside more obviously spiritual activities, such as prayer, to serve the needs of others as a form of spiritual practice.

Monastic Rules

As monasticism developed further, formal rules gradually appeared. As already noted, in circa 320 CE, Pachomius founded the first-known large monastic community at Tabennisis. He is also credited with writing the first monastic rule. This had a significant influence on the later Rule of St. Basil in the East and Rule of St. Benedict in the West. The adoption of rules codified the monastic way of life and outlined the hierarchy to which the individual should give obedience. This approach provided a vehicle of continuity but, equally, moved away from the spontaneity of obedience to a spiritual father or mother. Obedience was now to a rule of which the superior was the spiritual interpreter and legal monitor. In general terms, rules are normative texts that set out the spiritual principles guiding communities. However, a monastic rule is not essentially a legislative document but is a medium for the communication of a spiritual vision.

Although I want to focus particularly on significant aspects of the Rule of St. Benedict as an expression of the Way of Discipline, we

[13] Ibid., 180, number 18.

should briefly note the existence of other historic rules, such as the Rule of St. Augustine in the West and the Eastern Rule of St. Basil. Briefly, the latter derives from Basil the Great (ca. 330–379), one of the theologians known as the Cappadocian Fathers who bequeathed to Eastern monasticism its ongoing ethos.[14] The Rule (the *Asceticon*) is fundamentally an anthology of advice. Even during Basil's lifetime, several versions of the *Asceticon* were in circulation and questions of authenticity are complex. The Small *Asceticon* is the earliest version and probably influenced the Western Rule of St. Benedict. The most widespread form, known as the Great *Asceticon*, has influenced most modern translations. The tone of Basil's Rule is strict yet also relatively moderate when compared to early desert asceticism. The emphasis is on community life and a balance of liturgy, manual labor, and other tasks. Basil's vision of monasticism is also pastoral, and so provision is made for the education of children and the care of the poor.

The Rule of St. Benedict

The Rule of St. Benedict, written in sixth-century Italy, became the most influential monastic guide in the Western Church, influencing a broad spectrum of monasteries of both men and women as well as underpinning later monastic movements, such as the Cistercians in the twelfth century.

The Rule of St. Benedict draws upon the Rule of St. Basil, the Rule of St. Augustine (the earliest Western monastic rule), and probably what is known as the Rule of the Master. Another major influence was John Cassian, who became familiar with desert monasticism in Egypt. By around 420 he had settled near Marseilles, where he composed two famous works on monastic life, the *Institutes* and the *Conferences*.[15]

Given his iconic status in Western monasticism, remarkably little is known about Benedict of Nursia apart from the fact that he lived

[14] For a translation of and commentary on key passages of St. Basil's Rules, see Augustine Holmes, OSB, *A Life Pleasing to God: The Spirituality of the Rules of St. Basil* (London: Darton, Longman & Todd, 2000).

[15] See the translations by Colm Luibheid, *John Cassian: Conferences*, Classics of Western Spirituality (Mahwah, NJ: Paulist Press, 1985).

in the mid-sixth century, reputedly founded the abbey of Monte Cassino, and compiled a monastic rule.[16] While the Rule of St. Benedict (RB) is characterized by relative moderation and balance, it also presupposes a life of withdrawal from the public world. The Rule is also detailed and programmatic rather than an overt collection of spiritual wisdom. Its popularity is partly explained by a well-organized structure and the priority given to good order. However, its spiritual success also relates to a healthy balance of work, prayer, and rest and the creative tension between the values of the individual spiritual journey and of common life under the authority of an abbot.

Apart from noting the spiritual principles embodied in the three classic Benedictine vows of obedience, stability, and *conversatio morum*, I will focus briefly on the spiritual values of silence and listening, prayer and contemplation, and hospitality to the stranger.

Silence and Listening

The opening word of the Prologue to the Rule of St. Benedict is "Listen"—*Obsculta*. "Listen, O my son, to the teachings of your master, and turn to them with the ear of your heart. Willingly accept the advice of a devoted father and put it into action. Thus you will return by the labor of obedience to the one from whom you drifted through the inertia of disobedience" (RB Prol. 1-2).[17] This sets the tone for the whole Rule and its approach to the spiritual life. At the heart of the spiritual journey lies a commitment to listening in search of true

---

[16] Most of the details of Benedict's life come from the *Dialogues* of Pope Gregory the Great in the late sixth century. Gregory greatly promoted the "Benedictine way" without perhaps being technically himself a Benedictine monk. There are several good editions of the Rule of St. Benedict with translations and scholarly commentaries, and one of the best is Terrence G. Kardong, ed., *Benedict's Rule: A Translation and Commentary* (Collegeville, MN: Liturgical Press, 1996). For reliable and accessible introductions to Benedictine spirituality and the Rule, see Columba Stewart, OSB, *Prayer and Community: The Benedictine Tradition*, Traditions of Christian Spirituality (London: Darton, Longman & Todd, 1998); see also Esther de Waal, *Seeking God: The Way of St. Benedict* (Collegeville, MN: Liturgical Press, 1984). A classic study of monastic theology and culture remains: Jean Leclercq, OSB, *The Love of Learning and the Desire for God: A Study of Monastic Culture*, new ed. (New York: Fordham University Press, 2003).

[17] Kardong, *Benedict's Rule*.

wisdom. For this to happen, we also need to learn silence. In this silence we are able to cultivate attentiveness so that we are capable of becoming what we are not and receiving what we do not yet possess. Silence counteracts the human tendency to rush to angry judgment and destructive words. The Rule, of course, is full of scriptural quotations and resonances, and a broad analysis of the Bible shows that "listening" or "hearing" takes precedence over activity.

Listening implies being silent in order to learn or to be taught. The chapter of the Rule on silence, chapter 6, "De Taciturnitate," reinforces this. Interestingly, the word used is *taciturnitas*, "restraint of speech," rather than *silentium*, or quiet. That is to say that silence, literally "being taciturn," consists not merely of the absence of noise or in being quiet but in being sparing about what one asserts and in being receptive. This is the opposite of being domineering.

Silence also involves keeping one's mouth firmly closed so that the evil thoughts or lies in our hearts may not issue forth. In this discipline, we may slowly be converted to a gracious heart.

The spiritual quality of silence is closely related to the building of community because it implies a refusal to engage in polemic, which the Rule considers unchristian. The Rule implies that acceptable speech in community should always be modest and reasonable. Other monastic texts talk of silence as a necessary preparation for speech that is meaningful rather than ill thought out in terms of its consequences.[18] Do not rush to speak, the texts say, or to assert; above all, avoid speaking out of anger. By implication, all good speech is informed by contemplation—of God above all, but also, by extension, in a contemplative attentiveness to one another. The point is that silence and listening are part of the process of good communication.

The monastic tradition from its desert origins has witnessed to the truth that it is important to take care with words. Language without thought can be misunderstood and destructive. "One of the old men said, 'In the beginning, when we came together, we spoke to the good of souls, we advanced and ascended to heaven; now when we come

---

[18] On the different interpretations of silence in monastic writers and among those leading the canonical life, see Caroline Walker Bynum, *Jesus as Mother: Studies in the Spirituality of the High Middle Ages* (Berkeley: University of California Press, 1984), chapter 1.

together we fall into slander, and we drag one another to hell.' "[19] A key to monastic spirituality is the centrality of discernment, and this applies, above all, to speech. This enables a person to distinguish between language that is destructive and language that brings life. Words, most of all, only have value if they are the external expression of a life of integrity. Another early desert text records that an old man said, "Spiritual work is essential, it is for this we have come to the desert. It is very hard to teach with the mouth that which one does not practise in the body."[20] In summary, silence is not antisocial, nor a form of self-punishment, but a reticence necessary in order to be attentive and also to correct unproductive speech. The Rule of St. Benedict notes that vulgarity, gossip, and talk leading to laughter are forbidden in all places within the monastery (RB 6.8).

Obedience, Stability, and *Conversatio Morum*

Listening or attentiveness is associated with true wisdom, and this, in turn, is connected not only with our relationship to God but also to the notion of obedience. This is one of the three monastic vows, along with stability and *conversatio morum* (RB 58.17). Listening and obedience are intertwined.

Both listening and obedience are first of all to God, then to the spiritual master (presumably the writer of the Rule), to the Rule itself, and, in practical ways, to the abbot and more broadly to the monastic community. After all, the Latin verb on which the word *obedience* is based is *obedire*, from the two words *ob* (to) and *audire* (to listen or hear). So obedience is literally "to give ear to," "to pay attention to," "to listen to." Listen attentively to your brethren, for it is here that God speaks. Here, in the words of the Rule (Prol. 45), is the "school of the Lord's service"—a school of discernment and wisdom. Listening, connected to obedience, implies giving oneself wholeheartedly, rather than conditionally, to the common enterprise.

Apart from its emphasis on obedience, related to humility, as the primary image of spiritual progress (RB 7.31-55), the Rule also embodies spiritual values in the other two monastic vows. Stability is

---

[19] Benedicta Ward, *The Wisdom of the Desert Fathers* (Oxford: Fairacres, 1986), no. 106.

[20] Ward, *The Wisdom of the Desert Fathers*, no. 108.

related to the spiritual value of faithfulness. In the same way that early desert asceticism emphasized staying in one's cell, Benedictine stability is expressed by physically staying in the monastery—or remaining loyal to it and closely associated with it—until death. The third vow, *conversatio morum* (literally "conversion of manners") is a particularly difficult concept to translate. It implies a common way of life, having dealings with others, a manner of conducting oneself. Fundamentally, it stands for an overall commitment to the monastic lifestyle, including deep conversion and spiritual development throughout one's life.

Prayer and Contemplation

The central task of the monk is common prayer or the *opus Dei*: "nothing is to be preferred to the Work of God" (RB 43). There are explicit references to prayer in common, the "Divine Office," in chapters 8 to 20. This is to be supplemented by personal prayer (chapter 52) and what is referred to as *lectio divina*, "prayerful reading" (chapter 48). While the content and process of such prayerful reading is not explicitly specified, the use of the adjective *divina*, "divine," would seem to refer to the nature of the text. This would have been understood primarily as Scripture but also possibly as patristic spiritual writings. Its remote origins lie in early desert monasticism, where the famous collections of sayings of the desert ascetics often mention meditating and ruminating upon Scripture. The process was later described in terms of dimensions or stages, particularly when the practice was given a more systematic framework during the twelfth century in the text *Ladder of Monks*, by the Carthusian monk known as Guigo II.[21] I will briefly outline an approach to this spiritual practice in the conclusion, where I bring the various types of spiritual wisdom into conversation with contemporary practice.

Withdrawal and Hospitality

Western monasticism differed in its approaches to "moving to the margins" and separation from the everyday world. However, even the moderate Rule of St. Benedict recommended that "the monastery

---

[21] For a modern translation, see Edmund Colledge and James Walsh, eds., *Guigo II*.

should, if possible, be so constructed that within it all necessities, such as water, mill and garden are contained, and the various crafts are practiced. Then there will be no need for the monks to roam outside, because this is not at all good for their souls" (RB 66.6-7).[22] Almost universally, in pursuit of contemplative solitude, monastic property was situated in such a way as to avoid persistent contact with the outside world.

However, interestingly, in chapter 4 of the Rule, "The Tools for Good Works," withdrawal from the wider world is expressed in terms of living out different values expressed in different behavior. "Your way of acting should be different from the world's way; the love of Christ must come before all else. You are not to act in anger or nurse a grudge. Rid your heart of all deceit. Never give a hollow greeting of peace or turn away when someone needs your love. Bind yourself to no oath lest it prove false, but speak the truth with heart and tongue" (RB 4.20-28). In the same chapter, verse 8, the scriptural injunction to honor father and mother is changed to "honor everyone," presumably because a critical element of monastic values was to stand aside from conventional social and family obligations.

Despite the notion of physical separation and standing aside from conventional ties, the Rule is not rigid about physical withdrawal, as it lists among the work of the monks items outside the enclosure, such as injunctions to relieve the lot of the poor, clothe the naked, visit the sick, bury the dead, go to help the troubled, and console the suffering (RB 4.10-19). This attention to human need also extended to a major spiritual value—that of hospitality to the stranger.

Part of the historical witness of Christian monasticism as an "alternative society" was a new vision of human solidarity expressed especially in hospitality to strangers. The literature associated with the fourth- and fifth-century Egyptian desert ascetics offers numerous examples of charity and hospitality as a central rule of life. "A brother went to see an anchorite and as he was leaving said to him, 'Forgive me, abba, for having taken you away from your rule.' But the other answered him, 'My rule is to refresh you and send you away in peace.'"[23]

---

[22] Unless otherwise noted, quotations of the Rule of St. Benedict are from Timothy Fry, ed., *The Rule of Saint Benedict 1980* (Collegeville, MN: Liturgical Press, 1981).

[23] Ward, *The Wisdom of the Desert Fathers*, no. 151.

The virtue of hospitality offers a critical stance in relation to the normal ordering of society. Chapter 53, verse 1, of the Rule of St. Benedict states that all guests who arrive are to be received as Christ—"Omnes supervenientes hospites tamquam Christus suscipiantur." However, it is important to note that the Rule goes on to say, "for he himself will say, I was a stranger and you took me in."[24] In other words, Christ is in the stranger. This implies a theology or spirituality of hospitality deeper than merely giving food and board to a passing visitor. Commentators have always noted the word *omnes*, "all." This portrays an inclusivity linked particularly to *strangeness*, or we might say "otherness," in contrast to those who are like us. *Supervenientes*, "those who arrive," underlines the point even more strongly. It literally means those who "turn up unexpectedly." However, this is not a question merely of those who did not warn us that they were coming, but those who are a surprise to us in a deeper and more disturbing sense. Close to the surface of the text is the understanding that Christians are not to be choosy about with whom they keep company. The word *hospites* is nicely ambiguous. It can legitimately be translated as "strangers" as well as the more straightforward "guests." The former sense is reinforced by the reference to Matthew 25:35, "I was a stranger, and you took me in."[25] Finally, the word *suscipiantur* literally means "to be received," but its deeper sense is "to be cherished." Thus, the stranger turns into someone who, while different from us, we learn to value as closely as one of our own kin or tribe.

It is interesting that the Rule makes it clear that the poor are particularly to be cherished. "Great care and concern are to be shown in receiving poor people and pilgrims, because in them more particularly Christ is received; our very awe of the rich guarantees them special respect" (RB 53.15). Hospitality is personal and face-to-face, even though it is surrounded by rituals. In the Rule, hospitality is actually a blending of inside and outside worlds. In other words, it creates a "between place." In this liminal space, those who are "other" are encountered and the socially ingrained differences of any particular time and place are transcended, even if only momentarily.

---

[24] Kardong, *Benedict's Rule.*
[25] World English Bible.

Augustine's Monastic Vision

As a brief appendix to the Rule of St. Benedict and its teaching on charity, there are also useful pointers to a more social vision in the collection of monastic texts known as the Rule of St. Augustine. The various texts that make up this Rule are the most influential Western monastic guidebook after the Rule of St. Benedict. Nowadays, the scholarly consensus is that the male version of the Rule, known as the *Praeceptum*, is genuinely by Augustine and dates from around 395 CE.[26]

In the *Praeceptum*, a monastery is intended to be an example to wider society. It therefore models a social way of life where certain virtues are highlighted. First, *fides*—faith or faithfulness—refers back to an important Roman civic virtue. However, faith here implies living according to faith in Christ. This is not merely devotional but has profound social implications. The life of a monastery (and, by extension, of the human community) was to be exemplary, witnessing to Christ by living according to his teachings. The model Augustine takes is the community of the first Christians in Jerusalem, as portrayed in Acts 4, who are described as "one in heart and soul [or mind]." This divinely rooted friendship embraces both love and goodwill or harmony and brings about authentic "society."

Second, there is *concordia*, living in concord. In the *Praeceptum*, Augustine takes this classical notion and radically expands it. For Augustine, living in concord modeled a new ideal of community. The Rule makes clear that within the monastic community, representatives of every social class should live side by side—rich and poor, educated and uneducated, nobility and workers. This deliberately breached the traditional, rigid class boundaries within which monks had been brought up. Status, distinctions, and differences were to be left at the door of the monastery. This was not a pain-free process. Those who came from poor backgrounds were not to take advantage of their links with monks from rich families, nor were they to boast of such grand associations. Conversely, monks from wealthy backgrounds were not to disparage their poorer brethren. Rather, they should take pride in living with them.

---

[26] For a scholarly edition of the Rule of St. Augustine, see George Lawless, *Augustine of Hippo and His Monastic Rule* (Oxford: Clarendon Press, 1987).

6. Nor should they put their nose in the air because they associate with people they did not dare approach in the world. Instead they should lift up their heart, and not pursue hollow worldly concerns. . . .

7. But on the other hand, those who enjoyed some measure of worldly success ought not to belittle their brothers who come to this holy society from a condition of poverty. They should endeavor to boast about the fellowship of poor brothers, rather than the social standing of rich relations. . . . [27]

The third social virtue expressed in the Rule is *bonum commune*, or seeking the common good. It is a virtue that seeks to pursue common ideals while honoring individual needs. We find our own good by seeking the good of the other, and together we are bound to work for the good of the whole. In Augustine's ideal of community, the common good is the highest good of all. Nevertheless, Augustine wishes to allow for the uniqueness of each member. Each person should examine one's desires and aspirations in order to judge whether the needs of other people and of the whole might demand a degree of self-forgetfulness. Thus, in the Rule there is space for individual differences and needs.[28] "In this way, let no one work for himself alone, but all your work shall be for the common purpose, done with greater zeal and more concentrated effort than if each one worked for his private purpose. The Scriptures tell us: 'Love is not self-seeking.' We understand this to mean: the common good takes precedence over the individual good, the individual good yields to the common good."[29]

Thomas Merton and Monastic Spirituality

Thomas Merton (1915–1968), the famous American Cistercian monk, is arguably one of the greatest twentieth-century spiritual writers. He offers a challenging rereading of monastic withdrawal and an interesting conclusion to my reflections on the Way of Discipline. Merton's continued popularity lies in the fact that he wrote in

---

[27] Lawless, *Augustine of Hippo,* chapter 1, sections 6 and 7, 83.
[28] Lawless, *Augustine of Hippo,* chapter 1, section 3, 81.
[29] Lawless, *Augustine of Hippo,* chapter 5, section 2, 95.

a time of critical cultural and political change in the West, after World War II. In particular, the later Merton had an iconic role in a time of cultural and religious transition—a Catholic Church renewing itself through the Second Vatican Council, the encounter between Christianity and other world religions—particularly Buddhism—plus a time of critical political and social upheaval.[30] In a real sense, Merton is a paradigm of the late-twentieth-century spiritual quest. He stands for a movement away from a world-rejecting spirituality to one that embraced the outer world in all its complexity. There is a clear shift of perspective from Merton's traditional spirituality in his early book *The Seven Storey Mountain* (1948) to his radical comments on the public world in *Conjectures of a Guilty Bystander* (1966).

To a notable extent (explicit in *The Seven Storey Mountain*, *The Sign of Jonas*, and his diaries), autobiography was Merton's chosen medium for writing, even when the focus was not really on himself but on monastic spirituality or a spirituality of social engagement. Merton's focus on the self is in many respects one of the greatest attractions to readers in the late twentieth and early twenty-first centuries. One of his most striking counterintuitive moves was to suggest, by his lifestyle and his writings, that we need to step aside from the expectations of society in order to seek our mysterious inner depths. Merton positively sought another kind of self—a hidden, real self—capable of true dialogue and genuine encounter because it is not preoccupied with survival or self-importance.

What is countercultural about Merton's quest for "the self" is his growing conviction, in the face of a prevailing individualistic culture, that the self only truly exists in solidarity with others. Merton's later vulnerable self was no longer protected behind conventional monastic walls of separation and spiritual superiority. That was an important aspect of his second "conversion experience" in a trip to downtown Louisville. "This sense of liberation from an illusory difference [between monastic life and ordinary people] was such a relief and such a joy to me that I almost laughed out loud. And I suppose my happiness could have taken form in these words. 'Thank God,

---

[30] See Jean Leclercq, preface to Thomas Merton, *Contemplation in a World of Action* (New York: Doubleday Image, 1973), 12.

thank God that I *am* like other men; that I am only a man among others.' To think that for sixteen or seventeen years I have been taking seriously this pure illusion that is implicit in so much of our monastic thinking!"[31]

When Merton entered the Abbey of Gethsemani during World War II and published *The Seven Storey Mountain* in 1948, his presuppositions were in terms of monastery versus world. At that point, "the world" for Merton was a prison, framed by human egotism, evil and violent. At the opposite pole was the monastic-contemplative life. However, by the time of his *Life and Holiness* Merton was writing in very different language: "The spiritual life is not a life of quiet withdrawal, a hothouse growth of artificial ascetic practices beyond the reach of people living ordinary lives. It is in the ordinary duties and labours of life that the Christian can and should develop his spiritual union with God. . . . Christian holiness in our age means more than ever the awareness of our common responsibility to cooperate with the mysterious designs of God for the human race."[32] Merton gradually came to understand that a monk is not a person who simply withdrew from the world but rather someone whose contemplative solitude was a radically other way of being *in* the world with a responsibility for it. Part of Merton's renewed countercultural, prophetic stance involved opposition to the Vietnam War and support for the civil rights movement.

The later Merton interpreted the classic monastic *fuga mundi*, or "flight from the world," not as rejection of the everyday world but as detachment from materialistic values. To be countercultural is, in this way of thinking, to deny falsehood and to affirm whatever is good and true in human life. If monasticism involves a move to the margins, this becomes a means of solidarity with social and political marginality.

Fuga mundi, as a process of "standing on the edges," is not only a way of solidarity but also opens up the possibility of prophetic speech. In the title of his last journal, the posthumous diary for 1964

---

[31] Thomas Merton, *Conjectures of a Guilty Bystander* (New York: Doubleday, 1966), 141.

[32] Thomas Merton, *Life and Holiness* (New York: Doubleday Image, 1964), 9–10.

to 1965, *A Vow of Conversation*,[33] Merton plays on the double meaning of the classic monastic vow of *conversatio morum*. This is not only conversion but also speech.[34] On Merton's reading, *conversatio* implies not only a commitment to live in community with others but also living in "conversation." *Conversatio*, as central to the monastic way, is not only a commitment to the contemplative life but also, as Merton progressed in monastic life, a "turning to" the world in order to engage in prophetic conversation with it.

Merton's later approach to the marginality of monasticism was to see it as a vulnerable act of solidarity with other marginal people. The contemplative monk was to be a kind of social and political critic. The questions this raises are challenging. Will monasticism retain its prophetic freedom? Will monasticism be capable of standing for human solidarity against the privatization of life and spirituality? Will monasticism be able to reinterpret its long tradition of spiritual warfare in terms of a struggle against the powers of darkness in the world? Finally, will monasticism retain its visionary quality where the monk is called to learn how to "see truly" and by this to become an agent for the unmasking of illusion?

In other words, the contemplative has a strange and paradoxical power to confront the world of false consciousness. For Merton, the unmasking of illusion came to be the special mark of the monk. Through solitude and inner struggle, the monk listens deeply to the hidden voices of the world.[35] Merton was particularly struck by the meditations of Alfred Delp, the German Jesuit imprisoned and executed by the Nazis. His comments show how he shared Delp's sense that solitude, silence, and contemplation were the contexts in which the great issues facing humankind are worked through. Authentic contemplation confronts us with reality, and Merton was clear that

[33] Thomas Merton, *A Vow of Conversation: Journals 1964–65*, ed. Naomi Button Stone (New York: Farrar Strauss Giroux, 1988).

[34] This play on words is affirmed by Merton's editor, Naomi Burton Stone, in her preface to *A Vow of Conversation*, x–xi. The notion that Merton sought to link the vow to speaking to the world is also noted in Lawrence S. Cunningham, *Thomas Merton and the Monastic Vision* (Grand Rapids, MI: Eerdmans, 1999), 206.

[35] See Thomas Merton, *Contemplative Prayer* (London: Darton, Longman & Todd, 1973), 25.

this bore no relation to the narcissism of a bogus interiority that is an evasion of conflict and struggle.[36]

The Spiritual Values of Monasticism

"Monasticism" is not a single, simple reality. However, as an expression of the type of Christian spirituality that I call the Way of Discipline, it is possible to summarize some overall spiritual values.

The foundation of monastic spirituality may be described as "asceticism." While this implies a disciplined life, asceticism is not reducible to physical exercises or bodily deprivations. At its heart lies the notion of living in readiness for the kingdom of God, which is valued above everything else. In turn, this implies communion with God expressed in continuous prayer. Trust in God as the ultimate destination of the human journey demands singleness of heart as opposed to a divided heart. Everything that is extraneous to the search for God is stripped away in a life of simplicity, temperance, and frugality.

Contemplation is also a central value for monasticism, although it is not the exclusive preserve of the monastic way. Arguably, all humans are called to contemplation *by nature*. The same might be said about simplicity as a basic Christian virtue. This implies that monastic life is an exemplary form of Christian life rather than a substitute for ordinary human-Christian existence. Contemplation, in turn, demands attentiveness to God and, indeed, to the way God "speaks" through events and people. This attentiveness lies at the heart of the monastic practice of silence, in which one can learn the language of the heart and also cultivate the virtue of discerning wisdom. To live the pattern of contemplation-attentiveness-silence demands stillness rather than multiple distractions, and this is expressed in monastic teachings about the importance of stability. Stability is not simply staying in one place but, more importantly, is a matter of

---

[36] See Merton's commentary on Delp in *Faith and Violence* (Notre Dame, IN: University of Notre Dame Press, 1968), e.g., 52. On bogus interiority, see *Contemplative Prayer*, 135.

remaining focused rather than dispersed and of remaining faithful to, rather than distracted from, the demands of the spiritual journey.

While Christian monasticism embraces a variety of styles, from the solitary life to formally structured communities, the notion that monastic life overall anticipates paradise has been a frequent theme. For example, the stories of early desert ascetics sometimes explicitly speak of their life as a restoration of the harmony of paradise.[37] As Thomas Merton showed in his later writings, a "restoration of the harmony of paradise" has radically prophetic elements in the face of human violence, injustice, and social dysfunction.

Conclusion: Contemporary Developments

By way of a brief conclusion, it is interesting to note that the Way of Discipline, and specifically the ascetical-monastic path, has taken on new and imaginative forms in recent decades. First of all, there are new monastic movements within the Roman Catholic tradition. A notable example is the Fraternités de Jérusalem, founded in 1975 in Paris by Pierre-Marie Delfieux. This movement has communities of women and men living near each other in rented houses or apartments, in solidarity with their neighbors, and working part-time. Apart from sharing in their beautifully sung monastic liturgy of Offices and Eucharist, the groups of women and men seek to promote an imaginative reworking of the monastic desert in the heart of the modern city. New monastic ways of life have also emerged in Lutheran and Reformed traditions such as the Darmstadt Sisters in Germany and the women's monastic community at Grandchamp in Switzerland, which also has communities in France and the Netherlands.

Two ecumenical communities stand out: Taizé in Burgundy, founded by the Reformed Protestant pastor Roger Schutz, and Bose in Northern Italy, founded by a Catholic layperson, Enzo Bianchi. Taizé now numbers over a hundred brothers, both Protestant and Catholic, with an emphasis on fostering religious, social, and inter-

---

[37] See, for example, the notion of monastic life as paradise regained in "Life of Onnophrius" in Tim Vivian, *Journeying into God: Seven Early Monastic Lives* (Minneapolis: Fortress Press, 1996), chapter 7.

national reconciliation. There is a particular focus on young people, and more than one hundred thousand from different countries and religious traditions come on pilgrimage each year. Bose is a mixed community of men and women, again from different Christian traditions, who lead a life of prayer and work inspired by classic monasticism, Eastern and Western.

Finally, there is the diverse movement known as the New Monasticism, which, in some forms, seeks to foster a contemplative life in the everyday world without necessarily taking traditional monastic vows or living in structured communities. Some members of the movement are married, although there is an emphasis on nurturing new forms of a "common life." There is a strong commitment to peacemaking, nonviolence, ecological sensitivity, justice, and social reconciliation, fostering an attitude of hospitality and sharing economic resources with the needy.[38]

[38] See, for example, Rory McEntee and Adam Bucko, *The New Monasticism: An Interspiritual Manifesto for Contemplative Living* (Maryknoll, NY: Orbis Books, 2015).

CHAPTER THREE

The Contemplative-Mystical Way

My second type of spirituality, the Contemplative-Mystical Way, is associated with the desire for an immediacy of presence to God often linked to contemplative practice. It does not necessarily demand withdrawal from everyday life but suggests that this may be transformed into something wondrous. This way is often associated with an intuitive "knowledge" of God beyond reasoning and analysis. The ultimate purpose is spiritual illumination that connects us to the depths of existence. After briefly surveying the development of this way from the patristic period to modern times, I will take Julian of Norwich as a key example.

In popular writing, the word *mysticism* is often used nowadays to refer to esoteric knowledge derived from some kind of intense interior experience of God or the absolute. However, the more esoteric nature of the word has frequently been questioned in Christian theological circles precisely because it seems to bypass more rational approaches to religious knowledge in favor of the experiential.

One of the most influential twentieth-century writers about mysticism was the French Jesuit scholar Michel de Certeau (1925–1986). He can be credited with establishing that, as a distinct category related to experience, the noun *mysticism* ("*la mystique*" in de Certeau's words) seems to have originated in early seventeenth-century France.[1]

---

[1] See Michel de Certeau, *The Mystic Fable*, volume 1 (Chicago: University of Chicago Press, 1992).

However, the adjective *mystical* is more ancient. It comes from the Greek word *mystikos*. This describes the depths of Christian practice and theology. From roughly the second century CE, the word began to signify the hidden realities of the Christian life—for example, the deep spiritual meanings of the Bible and the inner power of liturgy and sacraments. Around the beginning of the sixth century CE, an anonymous Syrian monk, known as Pseudo-Dionysius, adopted the term *mystical theology* to indicate an engagement with the mystery of God. The main point is that "mysticism" is rooted in the call of every Christian through baptism to enter into the "mystery" of God through exposure to the Scriptures and to public worship.

According to Bernard McGinn, an important contemporary scholar and writer on Christian mysticism, mysticism consists of "those elements in Christian belief and practice that concern the preparation for, the consciousness of, and the effects attendant upon a heightened awareness of God's immediate and transforming presence."[2] "Mystics" are simply those who practice the Christian life with particular intensity.

Origins of Mystical Theology

The patristic theologian Origen of Alexandria (ca. 185–ca. 254) based himself on the classic neoplatonic threefold hierarchy of existence and knowledge. He suggested a threefold ascending pattern for spiritual progress associated with beginners (*praxis*), proficients (*theōria*), and the perfect (*theologia*). The spiritual journey was conceived as a recovery of the likeness of God in the soul in a movement upward from the material realm toward greater light.

Another patristic writer, Gregory of Nyssa (ca. 335–ca. 395), was a spiritual theologian of the highest quality, not least through his text of mystical theology, *The Life of Moses*. He also represented the contemplative journey in terms of stages of ascent but, in contrast to

[2] Bernard McGinn, "Mysticism" in *The New SCM Dictionary of Christian Spirituality*, ed. Philip Sheldrake (London: SCM Press, 2005), 19–25, quote at 19; in North America, see *The New Westminster Dictionary of Christian Spirituality* (Louisville, KY: Westminster John Knox Press, 2005). See also Bernard McGinn, *The Foundations of Mysticism: Origins to the Fifth Century* (New York: Crossroad, 1991), xi–xx.

Origen, the journey was toward darkness rather than light. His frame of reference was the story of Moses in the book of Exodus. Gregory's metaphor is the ascent of Mount Sinai, where Moses enters into deep clouds of darkness in his encounter with God. For Gregory of Nyssa, God is experienced in deep darkness but never conclusively known. The spiritual journey is never ending—a movement toward a perfection that we do not conclusively achieve during this life.[3]

However, the writings of the anonymous Syrian monk Pseudo-Dionysius around 500 CE were perhaps the single greatest influence on the development of mystical theology, East and West. He is best known in the West for his shortest work, the *Mystical Theology*, translated into Latin in the ninth century by the Irish theologian John Scotus Eriugena. This stressed that God is ultimately incomprehensible and beyond all names or affirmations. Consequently, God is to be "known" paradoxically by negating all conventional images. However, another treatise, *The Divine Names*, also dealt with God as revealed in the many names used in the Scriptures. The whole of Pseudo-Dionysius's spiritual theology is centered on the liturgy, which draws the believer into the pattern of divine outpouring and the reunion of created reality with God.[4]

Origen's and Gregory's expositions of the spiritual journey (allied with the writings of Pseudo-Dionysius) had a considerable influence on both Eastern and Western Christianity. During the Western Middle Ages, the conception of the spiritual journey developed strongly in the direction of what became known as the "three ways" or *triplex via* (purgative, illuminative, and unitive), which, while described in terms of consecutive stages, are more properly interweaving *dimensions* of transformation. Subsequent spiritual literature also employs metaphors for the spiritual journey—often the classic theme of ascent, whether of mountains, as in the sixteenth-century *Ascent of Mount Carmel* by John of the Cross, or of ladders, as in the fourteenth-century *Ladder* (or *Scale*, from the Latin *scala*—stairs) *of Perfection* by Walter Hilton.

[3] See, for example, Ferguson and Malherbe, *Gregory of Nyssa*.
[4] Colm Luibheid and Paul Rorem, trans., *Pseudo-Dionysius: The Complete Works*, Classics of Western Spirituality (Mahwah, NJ: Paulist Press, 1987).

Eastern Christianity

Eastern Christianity follows closely from patristic thought, which brings together theology and mysticism. Unlike later Western theology, the Eastern tradition retained a more unified approach in which doctrine, ethics, pastoral practice, and spiritual-mystical theory form an interconnecting whole. One of the most characteristic features of Eastern spirituality is the concept of *theōsis*, or deification, coined by Gregory Nazianzus, one of the Cappadocian theologians of the fourth century, and further developed by such figures as Maximus the Confessor in the seventh century and Gregory Palamas in the fourteenth century. *Theōsis* teaches that the destiny of humanity and of the created order as a whole is ultimate union with God-as-Trinity—indeed, to share in the divine life itself through God's grace.

In that sense, Eastern spirituality may be thought of as mystical—that is, focused upon the apprehension of and communion with the divine. One expression of this is "hesychasm" (from the Greek *hesychia*, quietness or stillness). From the time of the early desert fathers and mothers to the Middle Ages, the concept was virtually synonymous with monastic withdrawal and contemplation. However, the term gradually took on the sense of a state of stillness, reached through spiritual practice, whereby we can be freed from mental images as a prelude to union with God. By the late thirteenth century, influenced by monastic settlements at Mount Athos and Sinai and figures such as Gregory Palamas (1296–1359), hesychasm became a distinct tradition. The result, in part, was a growing emphasis on what is known as the Jesus Prayer (or the Prayer of the Name).[5]

Eastern Christianity, unlike Western teachings on prayer, was reluctant to emphasize method or technique. Nevertheless, the Jesus Prayer has been deemed particularly helpful in pursuit of inner silence and in deepening the Christian's intense relationship with the Son of God. In broad terms, it involves the frequent repetition of the phrase "Lord Jesus Christ, Son of God, have mercy on me a sinner,"

---

[5] On the Eastern spiritual tradition, see, for example: John McGuckin, *Standing in God's Holy Fire: The Byzantine Tradition* (London: Darton, Longman & Todd, 2001); John Chryssavgis, *Light through Darkness: The Orthodox Tradition* (London: Darton, Longman & Todd, 2004); Colm Luibheid and Norman Russell, trans., *John Climacus: The Ladder of Divine Ascent*, Classics of Western Spirituality (Mahwah, NJ: Paulist Press, 1982).

sometimes shortened to "Lord Jesus, have mercy," linked to our breathing. This approach to prayer is not simply a technique but involves complex inner transformation and demands careful guidance. This is clear from the nineteenth-century Russian narrative of an anonymous spiritual seeker commonly known as *The Way of the Pilgrim*, through which this tradition became familiar in the West.[6]

The hesychast tradition of spirituality was still further refined by Symeon the New Theologian (949–1022) and had a particular influence on the communities of monks that grew up on the Greek peninsula of Mount Athos.[7] While the tradition had its opponents, an important defender of the tradition, and a mystical theologian in his own right, was Gregory Palamas. Gregory entered one of the monasteries on Mount Athos and was thoroughly steeped in the hesychast tradition. His most famous work was the *Triads for the Defence of the Holy Hesychasts*—both an explanation and theological defense of the whole tradition.[8] Gregory affirmed that it was possible to experience the immediate presence of God. Additionally, Gregory believed, like Symeon, that the mystical experience of God might actually become a physical participation in the divine light itself.

Much later, in the eighteenth century, Seraphim of Sarov (1759–1833) was a profound mystic and became the most popular saint in modern Russia. Seraphim entered Sarov monastery in 1779. After monastic training and ordination, he lived for many years as a hermit in the forest in intense ascetical practice. He regularly received visitors for spiritual conversation. Eventually Seraphim returned to live in the monastery. He left his "Instructions," and his sayings were recorded by friends. *The Talks with Motovilov* became a spiritual classic. During these conversations, the phenomenon of transfiguration took place (that is, both people were surrounded by intense light). For Seraphim, the goal of the Christian life was the acquisition of the Holy Spirit. Those who attain the highest degree of the grace of the Spirit are transfigured. Seraphim taught a positive spirituality—a mysticism

[6] For a recent edition, see Aleksei Pentkovsky, ed., *The Pilgrim's Tale*, Classics of Western Spirituality (Mahwah, NJ: Paulist Press, 1999).

[7] C. J. De Catanzaro, trans., *Symeon the New Theologian: The Discourses*, Classics of Western Spirituality (Mahwah, NJ: Paulist Press, 1980).

[8] John Meyendorff, ed., Nicholas Gendle, trans., *Gregory Palamas: The Triads*, Classics of Western Spirituality (Mahwah, NJ: Paulist Press, 1983).

of light, joy, and resurrection. At the heart of his spirituality was the notion of the Holy Spirit permanently dwelling within each person.[9]

Medieval Western Mysticism

In terms of Western mysticism, two of the most significant groups of writers on mystical theology in the High Middle Ages were the Cistercians (a reform movement within the Benedictine tradition) and the Victorines (a version of the Canons Regular of St. Augustine).

The medieval Cistercians produced a substantial body of mystical writing. The eight volumes of treatises, homilies, and letters by Bernard of Clairvaux (1090–1153) is a classic expression of mystical-contemplative responses to Scripture, in contrast to the emerging "new theology" of the cathedral schools and later the universities. Bernard espoused an optimistic view of human nature and especially the innate human capacity for God. One of Bernard's most famous expressions of mystical theology is his *Sermons on the Song of Songs*.[10] Other Cistercians, such as William of St. Thierry (ca. 1075–1148), and English monks, such as Gilbert of Hoyland and John of Ford, continued the tradition of spiritual commentaries on the Song of Songs. This became a hallmark of Cistercian spirituality.

A striking aspect of Cistercian spirituality was the impact of women writers. A notable tradition of spiritual and mystical writings emerged from the nuns at Helfta, in Germany, who produced such spiritual giants as Mechtild of Magdeburg (whose visionary work *The Flowing Light of the Godhead* was written in the vernacular while she was still a Beguine), Mechtild of Hackeborn (*The Book of Special Grace*), and Gertrude of Helfta (*Exercises* and *The Herald of Divine Love*).[11]

---

[9] For texts related to Seraphim, including the conversation with Motovilov, see G. P. Fedotov, ed., *A Treasury of Russian Spirituality* (London: Sheed and Ward, 1981), 242–79.

[10] For translations of and an introduction to Bernard's writings, see G. R. Evans, trans., *Bernard of Clairvaux: Selected Works*, Classics of Western Spirituality (Mahwah, NJ: Paulist Press, 1987).

[11] For a good study of these Cistercian women, see Bynum, *Jesus as Mother*, chapter 5, "Women Mystics of the Thirteenth Century: The Case of the Nuns of Helfta." Two modern translations are Frank Tobin, trans., *Mechthild of Magdeburg: The Flowing Light*

Another important influence on the development of medieval mystical theology was the Abbey of St. Victor in Paris, where the Augustinian Canons Regular became known as the Victorines. They founded a contemplative-mystical tradition that combined Augustinian theology with the mystical theology of Pseudo-Dionysius and the new theology of the "schools." The two most important examples were Hugh of St. Victor (died 1141) and Richard of St. Victor (died 1173). Richard's doctrine was condensed into two important works, *Benjamin Minor* and *Benjamin Major*, which describe the contemplative journey. Richard and his disciples increasingly made their interpretation of the teachings of Pseudo-Dionysius a yardstick to judge the mystical way of life. Richard had considerable influence on Bonaventure's *The Soul's Journey into God* and on *The Cloud of Unknowing*, the anonymous fourteenth-century English mystical text.[12]

It is notable that the imagery of romantic, erotic love, as found in the Song of Solomon, offered a ready expression for a mystical spirituality of intimacy. In the writings of the Beguines this imagery became the basis for what is known as "love mysticism" or "bridal mysticism." The Beguines were a spiritual movement of lay women who generally lived together in groups without being enclosed like cloistered nuns and often combined contemplative practice with education and ministry to the poor.[13]

The mysterious figure of Hadewijch may be taken as a classic example of the mystical strand of Beguine spirituality. We know very little about her. Hadewijch was Flemish and was probably writing in the first half of the thirteenth century. She was clearly highly educated and familiar with the conventions of courtly love lyrics. She also appears to have been influenced by Augustine, the Cistercians, and the Victorines. Her writings include forty-five poems in stanzas, sixteen poems in couplets, thirty-one letters (both of spiritual guid-

---

of the Godhead, Classics of Western Spirituality (Mahwah, NJ: Paulist Press, 1998), and Margaret Winkworth, trans. and ed., *Gertrude of Helfta: The Herald of Divine Love*, Classics of Western Spirituality (Mahwah, NJ: Paulist Press, 1993).

[12] On canonical spirituality, see Bynum, *Jesus as Mother*, chapter 1. On the Victorines, see Steven Chase, *Contemplation and Compassion: The Victorine Tradition* (London: Darton, Longman & Todd, 2003).

[13] For an overview of the Beguines and their spirituality, see Sheldrake, *Spirituality and History*, chapter 6, "Context and Conflicts: The Beguines."

ance and spiritual mini-treatises), and fourteen visions. Hadewijch is one of the clearest examples of the Western tradition of love mysticism. Her writing pursues three basic themes: love (both as God's own nature and as the response of the human soul); the culmination of our relationship with God as entering an abyss (she even risks speaking of somehow *becoming* God); and participation in the sufferings of Christ. *Love* is the term that appears most prominently in her poetry. We can only embrace God through love.[14]

Another important figure in the development of medieval mystical theology was Bonaventure (1217–1274). He was a key person in the consolidation of Franciscan spirituality. Bonaventure was a theologian, a mystic, and head of the Friars Minor, the main branch of the Franciscan Order. Two years after his election as minister general in 1257, Bonaventure (later called Seraphic Doctor) spent some time at the hermitage of Mount Alverna, where Francis had had his own mystical experiences. Here Bonaventure came to understand that the spiritual journey of Francis was a model for others. This conviction, allied to his use of the mystical theology of Pseudo-Dionysius mediated through the Victorines, resulted in his greatest work of mystical theology, *Itinerarium Mentis in Deum—The Soul's Journey into God*.[15] Here, the contemplative way is open to everyone, women and men in the everyday world. The spiritual journey to union with God is expressed in the classic metaphor of ascent, with Christ as the ladder. It also combines the two characteristic Franciscan themes of contemplation of God indwelling in creation and intense love of Christ crucified.

Fourteenth-Century Mystics

The fourteenth century is particularly rich in major mystical writers. First, I offer some significant examples of key figures and writings. There are the so-called Rhineland mystics—the Dominican

[14] Columba Hart, trans., *Hadewijch: The Complete Works*, Classics of Western Spirituality, (Mahwah, NJ: Paulist Press, 1980).
[15] See Ewert Cousins, trans., *Bonaventure: The Soul's Journey into God, The Tree of Life, The Life of St. Francis*, Classics of Western Spirituality (Mahwah, NJ: Paulist Press, 1978).

Meister Eckhart and his disciples Henry Suso and John Tauler. Then there is Jan Ruusbroec, and finally there are two famous women, Catherine of Siena and Julian of Norwich.

Meister Eckhart (ca. 1260–ca. 1328), a German Dominican theologian and preacher, studied at Cologne and Paris and may have been taught by Albert the Great, from whom he gained a taste for the neoplatonic mysticism of Pseudo-Dionysius, balanced by the Aristotelian philosophy of Thomas Aquinas. Eckhart is the object of a great deal of contemporary fascination even beyond Christianity because of his paradoxical religious language. On the one hand, he suggests that there is an absolute abyss separating us from a transcendent God. This leads him to speak of the need for a "denial" of our concepts of God in order to touch the divine "ground" itself, what may be called the "God beyond God." On the other hand, Eckhart also made daring assertions of mystical identity between us and God. He is at his most radical in his vernacular German sermons. His obscure language led to suspicions of heresy and the condemnation of some of his teaching—although this is now generally thought to be based on misunderstandings.[16]

Henry Suso (1295–1366), another Dominican, trained at Cologne. He is the most literary of the Dominican trio and left many treatises, letters, and sermons, as well as an autobiography. Suso was directly influenced by Eckhart's ideas on negativity and on union with God in his *Little Book of Truth* but offered a rather different spirituality in his *Little Book of Eternal Wisdom*. This became a devotional classic and has strong elements of love mysticism and Christocentric devotion.[17] The third of the Rhineland Dominicans was John Tauler (ca. 1300–1361). He was born near Strasburg and, as a Dominican, was known especially for his preaching, available in a collection of some eighty sermons that later influenced Martin Luther. Tauler "translated" the

---

[16] Bernard McGinn and Edmund Colledge, trans., *Meister Eckhart: The Essential Sermons, Commentaries, Treatises, and Defense*, Classics of Western Spirituality (Mahwah, NJ, Paulist Press, 1985), and Bernard McGinn and Frank Tobin, trans., *Meister Eckhart: Teacher and Preacher*, Classics of Western Spirituality (Mahwah, NJ: Paulist Press, 1987). See also Bernard McGinn, *The Mystical Thought of Meister Eckhart* (New York: Crossroad, 2001).

[17] Frank Tobin, ed. and trans., *Henry Suso: The Exemplar, with Two German Sermons*, Classics of Western Spirituality (Mahwah, NJ: Paulist Press, 1989).

negative mysticism of Eckhart in terms of a more practical and active spirituality. He spoke of the eruption of the eternal into human life. The only adequate response to this was a continual process of conversion and a firm emphasis on humility before the otherness of God.[18] Eckhart, Suso, and Tauler developed a widespread network of relationships in the Rhineland and beyond, with laypeople, communities of nuns, and, above all, with groups of Beguines.

Another great fourteenth-century mystical writer was Jan (or John) Ruusbroec (1293–1381). He was the most substantial of the Flemish mystics. Ruusbroec was influenced by the Beguines and especially by the works of Hadewijch. Originally a parish priest in Brussels, at the age of fifty Ruusbroec began to live a secluded life at Groenendaal and founded a community of Augustinian Canons. One of his major works was *The Spiritual Espousals*, written while working in Brussels. At Groenendaal he built upon this in a number of other treatises, such as *The Sparkling Stone*. Like Hadewijch, Ruusbroec wrote of the contemplative union with God "without difference" as a communion of love. His love mysticism is more theological than devotional and is notable for a strong emphasis on the image of the Trinity in the human soul. Ruusbroec also strongly criticized any tendency to separate contemplation from Christian action, from ethical behavior, or from the sacramental life of the church.[19]

An important woman mystic was Catherine of Siena (1347–1380). She was an activist and visionary who at eighteen became a lay member of the Dominican Third Order, living at home. Her precocious spiritual life and extreme fasting (with anorexic overtones) has attracted unfavorable psychological interpretations. However, Catherine is equally notable for the richness of her spiritual teachings (expressed in many letters and in her *Dialogue*), for her hard work with the sick, poor, and marginalized, and for the impact of her public interventions to bring peace between Italian city states and to persuade Pope Gregory XI to return to Rome from Avignon. In the *Dialogue*, based on her experiences of contemplative union with God,

---

[18] Maria Shrady, trans., *Johannes Tauler: Sermons*, Classics of Western Spirituality (Mahwah, NJ: Paulist Press, 1985).

[19] James Wiseman, trans., *John Ruusbroec: The Spiritual Espousals and Other Works*, Classics of Western Spirituality (Mahwah, NJ: Paulist Press, 1985).

Catherine taught the positive power of human desire, which, she wrote, is one of the few ways of touching God.[20]

Julian of Norwich (ca. 1342–ca. 1417/20) is a particularly rich example of late-medieval mysticism. She is the first woman known to have written in Middle English, alongside Geoffrey Chaucer, in the so-called Age of the Vernacular. In the judgment of many, Julian was also one of the greatest English theologians and is the most original of the fourteenth-century so-called English Mystics who flourished during a period of immense social and religious upheaval including the plague (known as the Black Death), the Hundred Years' War, the Peasants' Revolt, Lollard heresy and, more widely, the Great Schism, when the Western Church was divided in loyalty to competing popes. The other major English Mystics were Walter Hilton, Richard Rolle, Margery Kempe, and the anonymous author of *The Cloud of Unknowing* and other works. As a conclusion to this chapter on the Contemplative-Mystical Way, Julian will be explored more fully as an important exemplar.

The Era of the Reformations

While the late medieval spiritual movement known as the Devotio Moderna (modern devotion), and the Reformation-era movements it inspired, may be said to have mystical elements, they will be considered again in the next chapter on the Way of Practical Action. That way more effectively expresses the dynamism of both the Protestant Reformation and the Catholic Reformation.

In relation to the mystical way, Martin Luther, for example, had an interest in medieval mystical teachings (such as Tauler) and taught a kind of mystical participation in Christ by faith. However, he rejected the neoplatonic emphasis on an ascent away from material existence.[21] Alongside John Calvin's practical, reform-oriented spirituality, he also had a sense of a mystical union between the believer and Christ. In some respects, Calvin shared with apophatic medieval mysticism a degree of skepticism about the capacity of the intellect

---

[20] Suzanne Noffke, trans., *Catherine of Siena: The Dialogue*, Classics of Western Spirituality (Mahwah, NJ: Paulist Press, 1980).

[21] See, for example, Philip D. W. Krey and Peter D. S. Krey, eds. and trans., *Luther's Spirituality*, Classics of Western Spirituality (Mahwah, NJ: Paulist Press, 2007).

to grasp the transcendence of God. As his *Institutes of Religion* suggest, true knowledge of God consists of a union of love. For God is not merely a judge of our actions but also gently attracts the believer toward divine love.[22]

The more radical spirituality of the varied Anabaptist movement also owed a great deal to late-medieval mystical movements. Like Luther, Anabaptists were influenced by Tauler. In particular, they drew upon and adapted the Rhineland Dominican's teachings about patient and trustful abandonment to God (known as *Gelassenheit*).[23]

Another strand of radical Protestantism, Puritanism, flourished in seventeenth-century England and later in North America, especially in New England. Puritanism was theologically Calvinist and empha-sized spiritual and moral renewal. The movement was never at home in the mainstream of the Church of England. A number of its central figures began as Anglicans but became "separatists." Puritanism's somewhat ascetical spirituality was offset in some people by a more contemplative-mystical stance. Thus, Isaac Ambrose derived some elements of his writings from the medieval Cistercian tradition of sermons on the Song of Solomon and also from bridal mysticism. Those sources were directly cited by Ambrose.[24]

In terms of the Catholic Reformation, Ignatius Loyola and the spirituality of his Spiritual Exercises is undoubtedly the best-known example. While emphasizing practical action and mission, Ignatian spirituality also encouraged a contemplative attitude. This was sum-marized in the distinctive idea of being a "contemplative in action." Ignatius himself witnessed to what may be called a "mysticism of practice" or a "mysticism of the present moment." However, after Ignatius' death there was a growing reaction against contemplative-minded Jesuits such as Balthasar Alvarez, Teresa of Avila's spiritual director. The subsequent history of the Ignatian tradition saw a nar-rowing of perspective. By the time the Official Directory for giving

---

[22] See, for example, Elsie Anne McKee, ed. and trans., *John Calvin: Writings on Pastoral Piety*, Classics of Western Spirituality (Mahwah, NJ: Paulist Press, 2001).

[23] Daniel Liechty, ed. and trans., *Early Anabaptist Spirituality*, Classics of Western Spirituality (Mahwah, NJ: Paulist Press, 1994); C. Arnold Snyder, *Following in the Footsteps of Christ: The Anabaptist Tradition* (London: Darton, Longman & Todd, 2004).

[24] See Tom Schwanda, *Soul Recreation: The Contemplative-Mystical Piety of Puritanism* (Eugene OR: Wipf and Stock, 2012).

the Exercises appeared in 1599, the official line was ascetical and methodical rather than contemplative. This narrow approach dominated up until the 1960s. The spirituality of Ignatius Loyola will be considered in more detail as the main example of the next chapter on the Way of Practical Action.

Carmelite Mysticism

A striking example of the Contemplative-Mystical Way in the post-Reformation period was the reform of the Carmelite Order in Spain and the mystical teachings that arose from it. The writings of Teresa of Avila (1515–1582) and John of the Cross (1542–1591) are among the greatest classics of Western mystical literature. Both were strongly influenced by the text of the Song of Solomon and the medieval tradition of "spiritual marriage."[25]

Teresa of Avila initiated the Carmelite reform movement with which John of the Cross became involved and which sought to return the order to its contemplative and semi-eremitical roots. Teresa came from a wealthy, partly Jewish family and entered the Carmelite convent in Avila in 1535. After some years of intense prayer followed by visionary experiences, she was drawn to a life of stricter observance. Having met a young friar called John of the Cross, she arranged for him to assist her. Teresa wrote a number of engaging works, such as her *Life* and *The Way of Perfection*. In her great classic, *The Interior Castle*, Teresa vividly describes the spiritual journey in terms of progression through the different rooms or mansions of the "castle" of the soul, clustered in groups corresponding to the threefold way, until the pilgrimage culminates in rooms five through seven. There, a transforming union takes place, leading to spiritual marriage. In one sense, her mysticism is orthodox, Christ-centered, and trinitarian. Yet her Jewish ancestry is nowadays more readily acknowledged, and the likely influence of Jewish mystical writings (especially *Zohar*) on *The Interior Castle* is also more freely suggested.

[25] See, for example, Kieran Kavanaugh and Otilio Rodriguez, trans., *Teresa of Avila: The Interior Castle*, Classics of Western Spirituality (Mahwah, NJ: Paulist Press, 1979); Kieran Kavanaugh, ed., *John of the Cross: Selected Writings*, Classics of Western Spirituality (Mahwah, NJ: Paulist Press, 1987); Peter Tyler, "Carmelite Spirituality," in *The Bloomsbury Guide to Christian Spirituality*, ed. Richard Woods and Peter Tyler (London: Bloomsbury, 2012), 117–29.

In contrast to Teresa, John of the Cross came from a poor family and was initially an apprentice craftsman. It is now thought that his father was also Jewish in origin. He received more education at a Jesuit school before entering the local Carmelite monastery. His encounter with Teresa of Avila changed his life. Like her, John was drawn into the reform movement. John's writings are denser than Teresa's and include mystical poetry of the highest literary quality and commentaries on the spiritual journey, such as *The Ascent of Mount Carmel, The Dark Night, The Spiritual Canticle,* and *The Living Flame of Love.* He emphasized a process of stripping away our desire for what is less than "everything." This stood in the way of union with God, who is "all."

> To reach satisfaction in all
>   desire its possession in nothing.
> To come to possess all
>   desire the possession of nothing.
> To arrive at being all
>   desire to be nothing.
> To come to the knowledge of all
>   desire the knowledge of nothing.
> To come to the pleasure you have not
>   you must go by a way in which you enjoy not.
> To come to the knowledge you have not
>   you must go by a way in which you know not.
> To come to the possession you have not
>   you must go by a way in which you possess not.
> To come to be what you are not
>   you must go by a way in which you are not.[26]

In *The Ascent of Mount Carmel*, John adopts the ancient metaphor of climbing a mountain to describe the spiritual journey. In John's case, progress was away from sense experience through various "dark nights" of spiritual darkness to a transforming union—a spiritual marriage between God and the soul. The impact of Al-Andalus Sufism on the language and symbolism of John of the Cross is now

---

[26] *The Ascent of Mount Carmel*, book 1, chapter 13, 11, in Kavanaugh, ed., *John of the Cross.*

proposed by some scholars, although the details are still debated.[27] Examples are the notion of ecstatic fire and burning flames of love in John's poem "Llama de amor viva" and the imagery of flowing water and the fountain of the soul in stanza 12 of *The Spiritual Canticle*.

As a nineteenth-century appendix to Carmelite mysticism we should briefly note Thérèse of Lisieux (1873–1897). Thérèse was a Discalced Carmelite nun in the Lisieux Carmel in Northern France. She was most famous for her "little way," which had a wide influence among lay Christians. However, she was familiar with the mystical writings of Teresa of Avila and John of the Cross and during the last year and a half of her life, while suffering from tuberculosis, went through a "night of nothingness" where she battled with spiritual darkness before breaking through to an intense mystical engagement with the present moment.

Seventeenth-Century Anglican Spirituality

The Church of England and the Anglican spiritual tradition that arose from it are a quite distinctive example of a church of the Reformation. It continued to display elements of pre-Reformation Western Catholic structures, liturgy, and spiritual practice. To suggest that the Church of England had no place for the mystical seems an unfair judgment when we read the sublime poetry of George Herbert and Henry Vaughan, the meditations of Thomas Traherne, and the overtly mystical concerns of the eccentric William Law in his early eighteenth-century *A Serious Call to a Devout and Holy Life*.[28] For example, Thomas Traherne's book of meditative reflections, *Centuries*, offered a mystical spirituality of joy in God's creation and of spiritual desire.[29]

---

[27] See, L. López-Baralt, *San Juan de la Cruz y el Islam: Estudios sobre las Filiaciones Semíticas de su Literatura Mística* (Madrid: Hiperion, 1990). Other scholars think that Baralt reads too much into the material but believe there may be some Islamic influences.

[28] Paul Stanwood, ed., *William Law: A Serious Call to a Devout and Holy Life, The Spirit of Love*, Classics of Western Spirituality (Mahwah, NJ: Paulist Press, 1978).

[29] For an overview of Anglican mysticism, see Bernard McGinn, *Mysticism in the Reformation: 1500–1650, Part 1* (New York: Crossroad, 2016), chapter 4, "Mysticism in the English Reformation."

The sophisticated seventeenth-century poetry of George Herbert is one of the best-loved expressions of the Anglican spiritual temperament. This will be considered in chapter 5, "The Way of Beauty," in which attention will be given both to his poetry and his interest in music.

The evocative meditations and poetry by the seventeenth-century Anglican priest Thomas Traherne have a clear mystical edge. Indeed, the mystical aspects of Traherne are underlined by the late Denise Inge, a modern Traherne scholar, in her introduction to an overview and selection of Traherne's writings, *Happiness and Holiness: Thomas Traherne and His Writings*.[30] Although, as Inge and other commentators note, much of Traherne's mystical sensibility relates to mystical union with the world, Traherne also had a deep and intense experience of God. He was convinced from his inner experience that God is a God of desire. Indeed, Traherne is one of the most beautiful spiritual writers on the subject of desire—God's and our own. First, there is his poem "Desire."

> For giving me desire,
> An eager thirst, a burning ardent fire,
> A virgin infant flame,
> A love with which into the world I came,
> An inward hidden heavenly love,
> Which in my soul did work and move,
> And ever ever me inflame,
> With restless longing heavenly avarice,
> That never could be satisfied,
> That did incessantly a Paradise
> Unknown suggest, and something undescried
> Discern, and bear me to it; be
> Thy name for ever prais'd by me.[31]

Then, in his prose meditations: "You must want like a God that you may be satisfied like God. Were you not made in his image? . . . His

---

[30] See Denise Inge, *Happiness and Holiness: Thomas Traherne and His Writings* (Norwich, UK: Canterbury Press, 2008) and *Wanting Like a God: Desire and Freedom in Thomas Traherne* (London: SCM Press, 2009).

[31] Thomas Traherne, "Desire," in *Selected Poems and Prose* (London: Penguin Books, 1991).

wants are as lively as his enjoyments: always present with him. For his life is perfect and he feels them both. His wants put a lustre upon his enjoyments and make them infinite" (Traherne, *Centuries*, 1.44).[32]

"You must want like a God." For Traherne, our human desire is actually the image of God within us, who is a God of desire. Indeed, for Traherne, God could not be God without desire because "want is the fountain of all His fullness." For, "had there been no need He would not have created the world, nor made us, nor manifested His wisdom nor exercised His power, nor beautified eternity, nor prepared the Joys of Heaven" (Traherne, *Centuries*, 1.42).

Seventeenth-Century French Spirituality

The mainstream of seventeenth-century French spirituality had some mystical dimensions. For example, Cardinal Pierre de Bérulle's Christ-centered spirituality mixed Dionysian mysticism with trinitarian theology. However, French spirituality overall, with iconic figures such as Francis de Sales and Jeanne de Chantal, had a more pastoral, mission-oriented approach than a mystical one. For this reason, more attention will be paid to it in the next chapter, on the Way of Practical Action. A striking, and controversial, exception was Quietism. In its strict form it was associated with the teachings of the Spanish priest Miguel de Molinos, and in a more moderate form with the circle of Madame de la Motte-Guyon (1648–1717). Guyon, fairly or unfairly, was associated with the notion of an excessively passive understanding of contemplation and with a total surrender to the initiative of God. Her works on prayer influenced such prominent figures as Archbishop François Fénelon and had a wide following. Guyon's teaching on prayer emphasized both affectivity and a kind of indistinct and objectless mystical contemplation. Guyon also followed in the long tradition of bridal mysticism (for example, her *Commentary on the Canticle*). What was open to question (and what ultimately led to her condemnation) was the notion of the soul's total "annihilation" in union with God and the lack of a solid sense of the salvific role of Christ in the spiritual life.

[32] Thomas Traherne, *Centuries* (London: Mowbray, 1975).

Ascetical and Mystical Theology

During the eighteenth century the Italian Jesuit Giovanni Battista Scaramelli (1687–1752), with his *Direttorio ascetico* (1752) and *Direttorio mistico* (1754), became the first person to establish a particular understanding of mystical theology that became common in Roman Catholic circles up to Vatican II. Scaramelli entered the Jesuit Order in 1706. His books became classics in the process of stabilizing a vocabulary of Christian perfection over the next two hundred years. The process of the spiritual life was conceived in two stages. "Ascetical theology" dealt with the form of the Christian life, based on disciplined practices, that applied to most people. "Mystical theology" analyzed the more advanced stages of the spiritual life up to mystical union. This applied only to an elite minority. Scaramelli was obviously more sympathetic to mysticism than many of his contemporaries, who were still nervous of Quietism. Indeed, he was forced to revise parts of his *Direttorio mistico* in response to serious objections.

Evelyn Underhill (1875–1941)

Turning to the early twentieth century, the notable author Evelyn Underhill remains a widely read writer on mysticism. Her motivation was to spread knowledge of the subject to a wider public. Underhill's most substantial book was *Mysticism*, originally published in 1911 and revised several times during her lifetime. Originally, she was somewhat preoccupied with esoteric religion and with neoplatonic suspicions of the material world. However, by 1930 this had changed to an interest in psychology, a closer relationship between mysticism and social awareness, and a greater integration of mysticism with the corporate life of the church. Her treatment of specific Christian mystics in the book was based on significant textual scholarship, and by the 1930 edition, her treatment of Christian mystics was relatively nuanced. While interested in comparative mysticism, Underhill did not describe mysticism as a category of pure "consciousness" separate from specific religions. She explored what was distinctive about Christian mysticism and was clear that this is practical in purpose.[33]

---

[33] See Evelyn Underhill, *Mysticism: The Nature and Development of Spiritual Consciousness* (Oxford: Oneworld, 1993); see also C. Williams, ed., *The Letters of Evelyn Underhill* (London: Darton, Longman & Todd, 1991).

Political and Liberation Spiritualities

Political and liberation spiritualities will be considered more fully in chapter 6, "The Prophetic Way." However, some examples should be mentioned here. African American author and theologian Howard Thurman (1900–1981) had a major influence on Martin Luther King Jr. and therefore on the civil rights movement. He is considered by some to have been a mystic. This applies especially to the intensity of his awareness of the unity of all things.

In terms of Continental Protestantism, during the late twentieth century the eminent theologian Jürgen Moltmann wrote about religious experience and the spiritual life. A notable example is his small book *Experiences of God*, especially the chapter "The Theology of Mystical Experience." There are interesting remarks concerning the distinction between mystical theology and doctrine. Moltmann also comments on the ethical dimension of "experiential wisdom" (*sapientia experimentalis*) that is associated with spirituality or mysticism. Moltmann's theology of the cross enables him to express the purpose of "mystical union" in terms that avoid any sense of a necessary transcendence of material existence. On the contrary, Moltmann perceives mystical union as a preparation for action, for radical political commitment, and for a deepened discipleship in the world.

Thus Moltmann suggests that in someone like Dietrich Bonhoeffer, murdered by the Nazis, the mystic becomes the political martyr: "The place of mystical experience is in very truth the cell—the prison cell. The 'witness to the truth of Christ' is despised, scoffed at, persecuted, dishonoured and rejected. In his own fate he experiences the fate of Christ. His fate conforms to Christ's fate. That is what the mystics called *conformitas crucis*, the conformity of the cross. . . . Eckhart's remark that suffering is the shortest way to the birth of God in the soul applies, not to any imagined suffering, but to the very real sufferings endured by 'the witness to the truth.' "[34]

Among liberation theologians, Segundo Galilea has written explicitly about the mystical and contemplative dimensions of political and social responses to injustice. There needs to be a movement away from the notion that an effective response to injustice is purely struc-

[34] Jürgen Moltmann, *Experiences of God* (Philadelphia: Fortress Press, 1980), 72.

tural and toward a truly spiritual experience of discovering the compassion of God incarnate in the poor. Humans are not able to find true compassion, nor create structures of deep transformation, without entering contemplatively into Jesus' own compassion. Only contemplative-mystical practice, allied to social action, is capable of bringing about the change of heart necessary for a lasting solidarity and social transformation. This is the heart of what Galilea terms "integral liberation."[35] Galilea calls for a reformulation of the notions of contemplation and mysticism. At the heart of the Christian tradition, he suggests, has always been an understanding of contemplation as a supreme act of self-forgetfulness rather than a preoccupation with personal interiority.

Conclusion: Julian of Norwich—An Exemplar

As noted earlier, Julian of Norwich is a particularly rich expression of late-medieval mysticism. For this reason, I want to end this chapter by taking her as an exemplar of the Contemplative-Mystical Way.[36]

We know very little about Julian. Even her name is taken from the dedication of the Norwich church where she became an anchoress sometime after a near-fatal illness in 1373, when she was aged thirty and a half. She had sixteen visions (or "revelations") of Jesus' passion over some twenty-four hours, provoked by the sight of a crucifix in her sickroom. Julian gradually came to believe that these visions, later expanded by God's further teachings and her own intense spiritual reflection over many years, were indeed revelations of how God sees reality and seeks to reassure humankind that God is love and only love. Julian's rich theological teaching is founded upon her intense mystical-visionary experience. Without this deep encounter with God, and the sense that she had been shown vitally important insights through that encounter, Julian would not have been provoked to write theology at all. In other words, Julian engages the

---

[35] See Segundo Galilea, "The Spirituality of Liberation," *The Way* (July 1985): 186–94.

[36] For a modern English translation see, Edmund Colledge and James Walsh, trans., *Julian of Norwich: Showings*, Classics of Western Spirituality (Mahwah, NJ: Paulist Press, 1978). For a study of her theology, see Philip Sheldrake, *Julian of Norwich: "In God's Sight"—Her Theology in Context* (Oxford: Wiley-Blackwell, 2018).

process of theological reflection and teaching with her lived experience of God and with her ongoing practice of a Christian life.

Julian's *Revelations of Divine Love* are available in a Short Text and in the more famous Long Text from which my citations are taken. This is a highly sophisticated work of mystical-pastoral theology written after twenty years of contemplative reflection. The only external evidence we have about Julian is an extensive reference in the autobiography of Margery Kempe, who visited Julian for spiritual guidance around 1413, plus several surviving wills, the last of which is dated 1416, that bequeathed money to Julian the anchoress.

The overall teaching of the *Revelations* is addressed to all Julian's "even christen" (fellow Christians). "In all this I was greatly moved in love towards my fellow Christians, that they might all see and know the same as I saw, for I wished it to be a comfort to them, for all this vision was shown for all men" (chapter 8).[37] For Julian, love rather than judgment or anger is God's reality. She begins with her visions of the passion. The point of these was to find in the broken figure of Jesus the reality of God. Thus, in Jesus Christ all humanity, creation, life, and eternal future are caught up into the very life of God-as-Trinity.

> And in the same revelation, suddenly the Trinity filled my heart full of the greatest joy, and I understood that it will be so in heaven without end to all who will come there. For the Trinity is God, God is the Trinity. The Trinity is our maker, the Trinity is our protector, the Trinity is our everlasting lover, the Trinity is our endless joy and our bliss, by our Lord Jesus Christ and in our Lord Jesus Christ (chapter 4).

From the vision of Christ on the cross Julian learned that everything is filled with God and protected by God. There is longing in God. "For as truly as there is in God a quality of pity and compassion, so truly there is in God a quality of thirst and longing. . . . And this quality of longing and thirst comes from God's everlasting goodness" (chapter 31). Because of God's painful longing for us, the longing we experience reflects God's own desire acting within us.

---

[37] My quotations are taken from the modern translation by Colledge and Walsh, *Julian of Norwich.*

In her teaching on Jesus as Mother, Julian is fully trinitarian. Thus, Jesus as Mother is not distinguished from the Father as Judge. Ultimately, the Trinity is our Mother. "And so in our making, God almighty is our loving Father, and God all wisdom is our loving Mother, with the love and the goodness of the Holy Spirit, which is all one God, one Lord" (chapter 58).

Julian also seeks to express something of how God sees. Because of this, she offers a radically alternative vision of creation, including humanity. She makes two striking assertions. First, there is no anger in God (chapters 45–49). Second, and related to it, sin is "no deed" (chapter 11). Julian sees all things in God and therefore "in all this sin was not shown to me." Later, as she considers how sin hinders her longing for God, she is taught that she could not see sin as she contemplated the passion because "it has no kind of substance, no share in being, nor can it be recognized except by the pain caused by it" (chapter 27). Sin is the cause of human pain and of the passion. Yet, in Julian's Middle English, sin is "behovely." That is, it is opportune because it enables God to show even more love. God does not "see" sin but only the bliss that will be ours. This is the ultimate truth of human existence, and so Julian, in her God's-eye view, cannot see sin even though she knows its effects within human life.

Needless to say, Julian found this very difficult. She struggled with how to balance her awareness that we sin and that the church affirms that we merit punishment with her inward understanding that God does not see us as fundamentally blameworthy. In anguish Julian cries out, "Ah, Lord Jesus, king of bliss, how shall I be comforted, who will tell me and teach me what I need to know, if I cannot at this time see it in you?" (chapter 50). As a response to her cry, Julian is offered the famous parable of the lord and the servant (chapter 51). This makes clear that everything depends on how we see. In the parable, the servant rushes to do his lord's will but falls into a ditch. There he does not see his loving lord, "nor does he truly see what he himself is in the sight of his loving lord." Indeed, as Julian suggests in chapter 52, "God sees one way and man sees another way." As the parable affirms, essentially God can see humanity only in the light of his Son. So, when Adam fell, "God's Son fell with Adam, into the valley of the womb of the maiden who was the fairest daughter of Adam, and that was to excuse Adam from blame in heaven and on earth." Finally, "in this our good Lord showed his own Son and Adam as only one man."

From this standpoint, the story of Adam (the Fall) and of Jesus Christ (the Incarnation) are to be seen as a single reality. The moment of Adam's fall becomes the moment of salvation as well. God looks upon us as we are "in Christ" and therefore sees us in our final integrity: healed, sinless, and glorified. In the light of eternity we are always in union with God. This is a theology of the irrevocable love of God, in whom there is no anger. The sinfulness and suffering of humankind is transformed by the re-creative work of Jesus our Mother into endless bliss. In Julian's words, despite the present pain of human existence, "all shall be well and all manner of thing shall be well." God will do a great deed—a mystery until the end of time because we cannot grasp it now. However, God's promise is that God will bring all things to good.

> It appears to me that there is a deed which the Holy Trinity shall do on the last day, and when that deed shall be done and how it shall be done is unknown to all creatures under Christ and shall be until it has been done. . . . This is the great deed ordained by our Lord God from eternity, treasured up and hidden in his blessed breast, only known to himself, and by this deed he shall make all things well; for just as the Holy Trinity made all things from nothing, so the Holy Trinity shall make all well that is not well. (chapter 32)

The revelations Julian received while seriously ill were not the end of her struggles. In the final chapter of her *Revelations of Divine Love*, she makes it clear that "I desired many times to know in what was our Lord's meaning." It was only fifteen years or more later that she received an answer: "And it was said: What, do you wish to know your Lord's meaning in this thing? Know it well, love was his meaning. Who reveals it to you? Love. What did he reveal to you? Love. Why does he reveal it to you? For love. Remain in this, and you will know more of the same. But you will never know different, without end" (chapter 86).

CHAPTER FOUR

The Way of Practical Action

My third type of Christian spirituality I refer to as the Way of Practical Action. This focuses on the spiritual potential of the present moment and the everyday world as the context for Christian discipleship. In this type of spirituality, we undertake practical action of various kinds in order to embrace a spiritual way of life. In other words, the Way of Practical Action asks us to respond to the call of God in Jesus Christ in a variety of radical actions in the world. For, in the words of Jesus, "the kingdom of God is among you" (Luke 17:21). Because this type of spirituality emphasizes seeking God in the world of ordinary events, it is more obviously a challenge to everyone and not simply to specialist groups dedicated to the ascetical life or with the opportunity for extensive contemplative practice. While I will end this chapter by focusing on one particular example, Ignatian spirituality, I first wish to outline a range of ways in which the values of this type of spirituality have been expressed across time.

The Scriptures and Christian Action

As with all forms of Christian spirituality, the theme of practical action has its roots in the New Testament. The foundational image for Christian spirituality is discipleship. Throughout the history of Christian spirituality, this concept becomes virtually synonymous with leading a Christian life. In other words, to be a Christian is to live in the world in an intentional way. As we saw in chapter 1, apart from "conversion" or repentance—turning away from sin—discipleship involves continuing Jesus' work of bringing God's kingdom into existence. "And Jesus said to them, 'Follow me and I will make you fish for people'" (Mark 1:17). The same call to active discipleship is present in the Gospel of Matthew (Matthew 4:17 and 19) and is implicit in the Gospels of Luke and John. Matthew 10 promotes a practical-active vision of discipleship: proclaiming the Good News, curing the sick, raising the dead, cleansing lepers, and casting out demons. Discipleship also involves the notion of service of others (in Greek, *diakonia*) as in the Gospel of Mark 9:35.

The proactive dimension of Christian discipleship is the task of extending God's kingdom to the whole world (for example, Matt 28:18-20, Mark 16:15, Luke 24:46-49). All forms of Christian spirituality are inherently connected to continuing Jesus' mission. However, it would be too narrow to understand the call to proclaim the kingdom simply in terms of preaching about God or of moral teachings about human behavior. Proclaiming the way of Jesus was understood from the start as living life after the manner of Jesus Christ. Thus, Christian disciples are to be a living message (for example, 2 Cor 3:3) by embodying the Gospel in a way of life, both individually and collectively. The history of Christian spirituality is a rich and varied commentary on how action and mission are to be understood as an important aspect of embodying a Christian life in the midst of specific historical and cultural contexts.

Missionary Monasticism

While the emphasis in chapter 2 was on monasticism as an example of the Way of Discipline, expressed by ascetical withdrawal, we should not overlook the fact that the history of monasticism also embraced active and mission-oriented elements.

As we have already noted, the period from the fourth to the twelfth centuries was one of major consolidation in the history of Christianity. First of all, Christianity emerged into the public mainstream as a result of the Emperor Constantine's edict of toleration (313 CE) and, within a relatively short time, became the official religion of the empire. Inevitably, this led to readjustments in self-understanding and in spiritual values. Partly as a reaction, new countercultural ascetical movements emerged and gave birth to monasticism.

In the context of the turbulent world of a collapsing Roman Empire, barbarian invasions, and the emergence of new kingdoms in Western Europe, monasteries became important centers for transmitting Greco-Roman culture to a postimperial world. However, monastic communities also became centers for missionary work during Europe's conversion to Christianity. Christian missionaries were often monks—for example, Augustine of Canterbury in England or the Englishman Boniface, who became known as the "apostle of Germany" in the mid-eighth century.

An important example was the emerging English Church, which was peculiarly monastic. Apart from Augustine of Canterbury's mission of Benedictine monks, dispatched from Rome by Pope Gregory in the late sixth century, it was Irish monks who effectively converted the bulk of the English, particularly in the Northeast, but also in the Midlands and even in parts of the south. The Irish model was of wandering monks who founded new settlements. Evangelization was really the result of, rather than the motive for, monastic settlement. In one sense, the primary motivation was spiritual and ascetical. However, it was characteristic of the wanderers to respond to any interest in Christianity among their new neighbors. For example, Columbanus and his followers effectively acted as missionaries across Europe as far south as Italy. In one of his letters to his followers, Columbanus indicates that "You know I love the salvation of many and seclusion for myself, the one for the progress of the Lord, that is, of His Church, the other for my own desire."[1] Interestingly, Adomnan's life of Columba on the island of Lindisfarne does not describe him as a missionary. Rather it is Bede the Venerable who gives this impression in his famous *Ecclesiastical History*. Indeed, he suggests that the missionary work of the monks of Lindisfarne was typical of the Irish Church.[2]

---

[1] For an overview of Irish monasticism and its spirituality, see Philip Sheldrake, *Living Between Worlds: Place and Journey in Celtic Spirituality*, 2nd ed. (London: Darton, Longman & Todd, 1997).

[2] See, for example, Bede, *Ecclesiastical History of the English People*, trans. Leo Shirley-Price, rev. ed. (London: Penguin, 1990), chapter III, sections 4 and 5, 148 and 150.

Medieval Active Movements

Later, during the twelfth and thirteenth centuries, the diverse *vita evangelica* movement of spiritual reform centered on a return to gospel values. This was expressed in simplicity, imitation of the poor and homeless Jesus, and pastoral action and preaching. The movement involved both men and women. In terms of a spirituality of practical action, two groups stand out. First there was the so-called canonical life, and second there were the mendicant communities. Finally, later in the Middle Ages, spiritual movements known as the Devotio Moderna and Christian humanism emphasized the cultivation of spiritual aspirations by lay Christians and also the importance of education.

An important spiritual movement with an active-practical emphasis was pursued by groups of clergy or women who lived in community as canons or canonesses regular, yet exercised a pastoral ministry. Many of these new communities of men and women ministered to the poor, nursed the sick, or cared for pilgrims. Some male communities took on the pastoral care of whole geographical areas. Other canonical communities integrated pastoral care with contemplative-monastic observance. For example, the Canons Regular of Prémontré (Premonstratensians) were influenced by elements of Cistercian austerity and, as we saw in chapter 3, the Canons of St. Victor in Paris (or Victorines) became notable for the foundation of a contemplative-mystical tradition based on the mystical theology of Pseudo-Dionysius.[3]

Later, the notion of mendicancy or begging for alms was a particular characteristic of many of the new religious groups of the thirteenth century. Eventually this way of life solidified into a number of new religious communities whose male members were popularly known as friars (from the Latin *fratres*, "brothers"). The most significant groups were the Franciscans, founded by Francis of Assisi in 1208/9; the Dominicans, founded in France in 1215 by the Spaniard Dominic de Guzman; the Carmelites, whose origins can be traced back to hermits in the Holy Land; the Augustinian (Austin) Friars,

---

[3] On canonical spirituality in general, see Bynum, *Jesus as Mother*, chapter 1. On the Victorines, see Chase, *Contemplation and Compassion*.

founded circa 1244; and, later in the fourteenth century, the Servite Friars, founded in Florence.

These communities emphasized poverty and itinerancy, following in the footsteps of Jesus and the early disciples, and popular preaching. In general the mendicant groups had their strongest influence on laypeople in the towns, with whom they developed strong spiritual as well as pastoral bonds. They not only engaged with the general population by preaching, teaching, and spiritual guidance but also built their churches with the spiritual needs of the city populations in mind. A large preaching nave often opened onto a city square that could accommodate even larger crowds at outdoor sermons. Surviving examples include the churches and adjacent squares of Santa Croce (Franciscan) and Santa Maria Novella (Dominican), founded at opposite ends of medieval Florence.[4]

In the later medieval period, the spiritual reform movement known as the Devotio Moderna was an important strand of spirituality that eventually fed into both the Protestant and Catholic Reformations. The Devotio Moderna flourished in Flanders and the Netherlands from the late fourteenth century onward. The movement represented city values and attracted both educated laypeople and reform-minded clergy. Its spirituality was an interesting mixture. It placed a strong emphasis on lay education and accessible meditative practices while also owing something to Flemish mysticism. An important figure in the movement was Gerard Groote (1340–1384), a deacon and popular preacher who advocated Christ-centered piety and supported moderate church reform. He produced spiritual writings addressed to laypeople and promoted education as the basis of a virtuous life. His educational method was person-centered and underlined the importance of both individual moral formation and the inculcation of a strong sense of community. Groote cofounded the Brothers of the Common Life, groups of clergy and laymen who lived in community without a rule or vows. Later there emerged equivalent groups of women, Sisters of the Common Life. The Brothers became involved in Groote's educational philosophy, sometimes running schools,

---

[4] For an overview of the mendicant communities and their spiritualities, see Jill Raitt, ed., *Christian Spirituality II: High Middle Ages and Reformation*, World Spirituality (New York: Crossroad, 1987), chapter 2, "The Mendicants."

acting as school governors, or administering parallel boarding hostels that offered spiritual guidance and tutoring. Interestingly, Martin Luther was partly schooled by the Brothers. The Devotio Moderna movement also promoted methodical approaches to prayer—for example, meditation manuals by Florent Radewijns and Gerard van Zutphen—which may have influenced Ignatius Loyola and his *Spiritual Exercises*. The most famous work of the movement was *Imitation of Christ*, attributed to Thomas à Kempis, which became a popular classic in both Catholic and Protestant circles well into the twentieth century.[5]

A second form of late-medieval spirituality that also placed an emphasis on reviving practical and social virtues was the movement known as Christian humanism. This offered a new ideal of the Christian life that also spoke to the world of Christian laypeople. One influential figure was Desiderius Erasmus (1469–1536), a Dutch priest, theologian, and reformer who was for some years an Augustinian canon regular. He promoted a serious, biblically based spirituality as part of his concern to reform the church. A major concern was the revival of Christian virtue. In this spirit he composed his famous book, the *Enchiridion* or *Handbook of the Christian Soldier*, plus editions of patristic texts and a critical edition of the Greek New Testament. With his English friends John Colet, the Dean of St. Paul's Cathedral in London, and Sir Thomas More, later lord chancellor of England and eventually a Catholic martyr, Erasmus sought to cultivate "the philosophy of Christ"—a biblically and ethically based spirituality. Erasmus died in Basle, having remained a Catholic in a predominantly Protestant city.[6]

The Reformation Era and Practical Action

During the sixteenth century, both Protestant and Catholic reform movements placed an emphasis on the importance of practical action as a spiritual principle. In terms of the Protestant Reformation, two

---

[5] See, for example, John Van Engen, trans., *Devotio Moderna: Basic Writings*, Classics of Western Spirituality (Mahwah, NJ: Paulist Press, 1988).

[6] A brief but good study of Erasmus's spirituality is the introduction to John O'Malley, SJ, ed., *Collected Works of Erasmus: Spiritualia* (Toronto: University of Toronto Press, 1989).

figures stand out in relation to a spirituality of practical action: Martin Luther and John Calvin.

As already noted in chapter 3, Martin Luther (1483–1546) had an interest in late-medieval mysticism. However, in many ways his spiritual principles fit best with the Way of Practical Action. As a young man, Luther was educated for a time at a school run by the Brothers of the Common Life and, therefore, presumably, influenced by them (and by the Devotio Moderna). In terms of the Way of Practical Action, Luther's eventual rejection of a hierarchy of spiritual lifestyles led him to a belief in the holiness of everyday life—work, family, and citizenship. All Christians have a single vocation through baptism, expressed in the notion of the "priesthood of all believers," which included ministering to other people. Although Luther rejected the notion that human works contribute to our salvation, he continued to affirm the value of good works as a sign of gratitude to God. The purpose of human "works" should be the service of others—a response to the needs of our neighbors in the concrete circumstances of daily life. Luther believed that the Beatitudes in the Sermon on the Mount were applicable to every Christian, in relation to both family and societal life, and not only to the monastic or clerical elite, to which Luther originally belonged as an Augustinian friar.[7]

John Calvin (1509–1564) originally trained as a lawyer in France and became sympathetic to Lutheran ideas while studying in Paris. He moved to Geneva, where he assisted with the Reformation movement until he died. In terms of Calvin's spirituality, one of his important characteristics was to engage strongly with civil society. In other words, for Calvin, spirituality was essentially a public-social matter. In the Christian city—for example, Geneva—what we think of as spirituality and citizenship should mutually reinforce each other. While Calvin's theology of human identity has sometimes been interpreted as individualistic, he insisted on the solidarity of human beings. Our neighbors, whom we should serve, include all of humanity. City elders and magistrates were not to be merely managers or lawyers but were also faithfully to oversee the covenant between the

[7] On the spirituality of Martin Luther, see, for example, Marc Lienhard, "Luther and the Beginnings of the Reformation," in Raitt, *Christian Spirituality II*, chapter 12, 268–99; see also Sheldrake, *Spirituality: A Brief History*, 115–16.

citizens and God. Overall, Calvin believed that the most praiseworthy life in God's eyes is one that seeks to serve society.[8]

In addition to the Lutheran and Calvinist mainstreams, there was also the Radical Reformation associated with the Anabaptists, whose name refers to their practice of adult or "believer's" baptism. This movement had no single identifiable founder and little structural organization. From around 1525, groups spread along the Rhine from the Netherlands to Switzerland, with other groups in Moravia and Austria. The tradition survives in communities such as the Amish, Mennonites, and Hutterites. The movement was often associated with withdrawal from wider society, radical simplicity, and even forms of family-based quasi-monasticism. However, the refusal to support political authority and opposition to the prevailing social order can be seen paradoxically as a way of practical action. Key examples are the widespread practice of sharing material possessions with those less fortunate and a philosophy of nonviolence and refusal to belong to military structures.

The English Reformation, while influenced by both Lutheran and Calvinist movements, was a more ambiguous and political process. It began in the reign of King Henry VIII (1509–1547) as a result of his divorce from Catherine of Aragon and stretched through a Protestant ascendancy under Henry's young son Edward VI, followed by a Catholic restoration under Mary, and ending with the compromise settlement under Mary's half-sister, Elizabeth I (1558–1603). Elizabeth's upbringing was broadly Protestant, but her own religious sensibilities were ambiguous or at least kept carefully private. Despite pressure to adopt a radically Reformed system, Elizabeth carefully maintained the historic episcopal system and Archbishop Cranmer's 1552 Book of Common Prayer with minor changes. The spirituality of the Church of England that developed after Elizabeth was shaped by the principles of the Continental reformers but also retained pre-Reformation elements and was open to aspects of Catholic Reformation spirituality (for example, the works of Francis de Sales and elements of the Ignatian *Spiritual Exercises*). The Church of England

---

[8] On the spirituality of John Calvin, see, for example, William J. Bouwsma, "The Spirituality of John Calvin," in Raitt, *Christian Spirituality II*, chapter 14, 318–33; see also Sheldrake, *Spirituality: A Brief History*, 117–18.

and the subsequent wider Anglican tradition had a strong pastoral-practical element. The Book of Common Prayer saw spirituality as implicitly shaped by living and worshiping in a community whose common life was both ecclesial and strongly civic. Residual Christian humanism, expressed during Elizabeth's reign in the writings of Richard Hooker, *On the Laws of Ecclesiastical Polity*, placed a high value on everyday human existence and on active participation in civil society. *The Country Parson*, a prose text on the personal and pastoral life of priests by the important seventeenth-century English poet and Anglican priest George Herbert, has a strong "practical action" dimension. George Herbert will be explored more fully in the chapter on the Way of Beauty.

In terms of nonviolence, another important group that grew out of the Reformed tradition was the Quakers (Religious Society of Friends). Nowadays, Quakers are a broad-based, spiritual-religious movement rather than one closely associated with conventional Protestantism. The movement originated in the teachings of George Fox (1624–1691), who found that conventional English Puritanism did not adequately address his spiritual quest. Fox believed in the presence of a divine Inner Light within every person. While this can sound intensely interior, this divine power eradicated human conflict. Authentic inner experience leads to a desire to seek the transformation of the social order. The Quaker movement is strongly ethical and includes a belief in peace, social justice, and nonviolence. A notable example was the work of William Penn, who sought to create the perfectly ordered society in Pennsylvania. In the United Kingdom during the Industrial Revolution, wealthy Quakers combined the foundation of factories with the provision of social care, decent housing, and schools for their workers. One notable example was the model town of Bourneville associated with the Cadbury family. During the nineteenth century the English Quaker Elizabeth Fry was a leading figure in prison reform, and during World War I and World War II Quakers were active as pacifists.

The Catholic Reformation

In terms of the Catholic Reformation, one of the most important spiritual figures—and certainly one who clearly expresses the Way of Practical Action—was Ignatius Loyola (1491–1556), author of the famous text the *Spiritual Exercises* and founder of the Society of Jesus (or Jesuits). Ignatius Loyola and Ignatian spirituality will be explored in more detail at the end of this chapter as a paradigm of the Way of Practical Action. In addition to the Jesuits, other new religious communities emerged to cater to the spiritual needs of increasingly educated and influential lay Christians. These new clerical communities, known collectively as clerks regular, emphasized in different ways a life of practical action.

Apart from Ignatian spirituality, the most striking spiritual movement of the Catholic Reformation was the reform of the Carmelite order in Spain. The writings of two key figures, Teresa of Avila (1515–1582) and John of the Cross (1542–1591), are among the greatest classics of Western spiritual literature and were outlined in the previous chapter. Their influential writings are most properly described as mystical, and the ethos of the reformed (or Discalced) Carmelites was fundamentally contemplative. However, the seventeenth-century French Carmelite Brother Lawrence (1614–1691) was a lay brother cook in Paris who also drew many people to him for spiritual guidance, including Archbishop Fénelon, an important figure in French spirituality. Brother Lawrence's letters and other fragments were edited after his death as *The Practice of the Presence of God*, which spoke of the possibility of union with God in the midst of ordinary, everyday tasks and practices.[9]

Overall, the spiritual development of laypeople was a major concern of Catholic reform. This led to the development of groups known as confraternities or sodalities, such as the Jesuit-inspired Sodalities of Our Lady that sought to combine prayer and everyday action, especially charitable work. In addition, a greater emphasis was placed by the new clerical groups, including the Jesuits, on the importance of preaching as a means of catechetical instruction and moral exhortation, and also to provoke spiritual development. This aimed to make lay Catholics more effective presences in the everyday world of work and social networks.[10]

[9] See W. McGreal, *At the Fountain of Elijah: The Carmelite Tradition* (London: Darton, Longman & Todd, 1999); see also Kavanaugh and Rodriguez, *Teresa of Avila,* and Kavanaugh, *John of the Cross.*

[10] See, for example, Philip Sheldrake, *Spirituality: A Brief History*, 135–37.

Seventeenth-Century French Spiritualities

French spiritual movements during the seventeenth century were also examples of the Way of Practical Action. There were three major groups associated with Pierre de Bérulle, Francis de Sales with Jane (Jeanne) de Chantal, and Vincent de Paul with Louise de Marillac.

Pierre de Bérulle (1575–1629), an aristocrat, theologian, and eventually cardinal, founded the French Oratory (inspired by Philip Neri in Italy) made up of communities of priests without formal vows. These focused their missionary work on preaching, education (including a school system inspired by the Jesuits), and reform of the clergy. In Bérulle there was tension between a Christ-centered and incarnational spirituality and a somewhat dark view of human nature that gave rise to a spirituality of abasement and servitude to God's will. A notable "disciple" of Bérulle was Jean-Jacques Olier (1608–1657) who founded the Sulpicians (Society of St. Sulpice). These, like the Oratorians, were a voluntary society of priests who founded seminaries with a view to improving the quality of parish clergy.[11]

Francis de Sales (1567–1622), aristocrat, lawyer, and eventually bishop of Geneva, had an extensive influence even beyond the Roman Catholic Church, especially via his spiritual classic *Introduction to the Devout Life*. Along with his close friend Jane de Chantal (a widowed baroness and founder of the Order of the Visitation), de Sales developed an approach to spirituality suited to both women and men living in the everyday world. Salesian spirituality appreciated the contemplative tradition but also emphasized service of neighbor, particularly people in need. Influenced by Ignatian spirituality, but with its own distinctive features, Salesian spirituality taught God's love for all humanity. One important theme was the heart of Jesus Christ mediating God to human hearts.[12]

The third important French spiritual group was associated with Vincent de Paul (1580–1660) and Louise de Marillac (1591–1660).

---

[11] See William Thompson, ed., Lowell Glendon, trans., *Bérulle and the French School: Selected Writings*, Classics of Western Spirituality (Mahwah, NJ: Paulist Press, 1989).

[12] See Francis de Sales, *Introduction to the Devout Life* (New York: Doubleday, 1982); see also Péronne Marie Thibert, trans., *Francis de Sales and Jane de Chantal: Letters of Spiritual Direction*, Classics of Western Spirituality (Mahwah, NJ: Paulist Press, 1988), and Wendy Wright, *Heart Speaks to Heart: The Salesian Tradition* (London: Darton, Longman & Todd, 2004).

From a poor background, de Paul was eventually ordained and dedicated his life to serving the poor, orphans, slaves, and victims of war. His spirituality was socially engaged rather than theoretically sophisticated. Union with God came through serving Christ in the poor. Vincentian spirituality was spread via communities of priests (the Congregation of the Mission or Vincentians) and communities of women (Daughters of Charity) founded with Louise de Marillac. Vincent's vision was also expressed in the development of lay confraternities dedicated to helping the poor in their homes.

Eighteenth Century—De Caussade and the Wesleys

During the eighteenth century, two examples of the Way of Practical Action particularly stand out: the French Jesuit Jean-Pierre de Caussade (1675–1751) and two brothers and Church of England priests, John Wesley (1703–1791) and Charles Wesley (1707–1788).

Jean-Pierre de Caussade was influenced by Ignatius Loyola but also by the sixteenth-century Carmelite mystics and Francis de Sales. De Caussade lived a relatively obscure life as a Jesuit engaged in spiritual guidance and was for some years chaplain to a community of Visitation nuns in Nancy. During his own lifetime, de Caussade was relatively unknown, publishing one anonymous work on prayer. The work for which he is widely known, and which has remained a popular spiritual classic, is *L'Abandon à la Providence Divine*, variously translated as *Abandonment to Divine Providence* or *The Sacrament of the Present Moment*. While modern scholars question his direct authorship, the work draws on his spiritual instructions and encapsulates his teachings. The book teaches a kind of mysticism of everyday life from which arises the notion of "the sacrament of the present moment." This involves discernment of the presence of God in everyday existence and an active response of self-giving and service.[13]

The work of John and Charles Wesley is associated with the origins of the Methodist tradition. Although the brothers remained Church of England priests, they represented a reaction against the formalism prevalent in the church of their day. Partly influenced by German

---

[13] Jean-Pierre de Caussade, *Abandonment to Divine Providence* (New York: Doubleday Image Books, 1975).

Pietism, John Wesley especially manifested a strong current of affective devotion in his life and work. While a Fellow of Lincoln College Oxford in the early 1730s, John Wesley gathered together a group of young men, known as the Holy Club, who cultivated an intense personal spirituality. Their disciplined regime of prayer and study earned them the nickname of Methodists—a name that eventually defined the societies the Wesley brothers founded to spread their spiritual reform. Apart from Pietism, John Wesley drew on a wide range of influences, including early church fathers, the Devotio Moderna, significant seventeenth-century Anglican writers, and also a number of figures in continental Catholic reform—for example, Francis de Sales and representatives of the French mystical tradition, plus a number of Jesuit works.[14]

In terms of the Way of Practical Action, John Wesley's interests went beyond personal holiness and included a desire to evangelize people who were untouched by the mainstream Church of England—particularly the working classes. Wesley was famous for missionary preaching journeys throughout Britain and Ireland. By the late 1760s the Methodist revival had reached North America. While concerned with personal, experiential faith, John Wesley fostered love and service of neighbor (particularly the poor and needy), and a spirituality that combined prayer and action. The universal need for salvation drove his missionary activity. Wesley assumed that his followers would continue to attend normal Church of England services, and he had a high view of the Eucharist, both theologically and in terms of encouraging frequent communion. Only after John Wesley's death did the Methodist movement become separate from Anglicanism.[15]

Nineteenth-Century Examples

In terms of the nineteenth century, the period after the French Revolution led to Catholic approaches to spirituality emphasizing

[14] On this question see, Philip Sheldrake, "The Influence of the Ignatian tradition" in *The Way Supplement* 68 (*Ignatian Spirituality in Ecumenical Context*) (Summer 1990): 74–85.

[15] On the spirituality of the Wesleys, see Frank Whaling, ed., *John and Charles Wesley: Selected Prayers, Hymns, Journal Notes, Sermons, Letters and Treatises*, Classics of Western Spirituality (Mahwah, NJ: Paulist Press, 1981).

the reconstruction of traditional institutions. Several historic religious orders were refounded, such as the Dominicans, and new reform movements appeared within other historical groups, such as Solesmes within the Benedictine tradition. However, there were also significant innovative developments.

In the middle of the century there was a major revival of Salesian spirituality. This was expressed in a new family of male and female communities plus lay associates founded or inspired by the Italian priest Giovanni Bosco, popularly known as Don Bosco. The revival placed a particularly strong emphasis on work with disadvantaged youth.

Another notable development was in the spirit of the lay confraternities founded in the seventeenth century by Vincent de Paul. This was the famous Society of St. Vincent de Paul founded by Frédéric Ozanam (1813–1853), a scholar and Sorbonne professor with a Jewish background. The society continues to flourish today as a large international voluntary organization of lay women and men dedicated to offering material assistance to the poor and needy. Ozanam was a key figure in the emergence during the nineteenth century of an active lay spirituality of ministry and service. In many ways this anticipated a wider development of lay groups after Vatican II. In recent times, the society has accepted members from beyond the Roman Catholic Church.[16]

Apart from the new Salesian family and the Society of St. Vincent de Paul, a number of new religious communities dedicated to practical action were founded. These tended to focus on work with the poor and on education. A notable example of the first is the Missionary Oblates of Mary Immaculate (OMI), founded in 1816 by Eugène de Mazenod (1782–1861). An important example of the second is the women's community known as the Religious of the Sacred Heart (or Religieuses du Sacré-Cœur de Jésus—RSCJ), founded by Madeleine-Sophie Barat in 1800. The community continues to play a significant international educational role at high school and university levels.

---

[16] See Frances Ryan and John Rybolt, eds., *Vincent de Paul and Louise de Marillac: Rules, Conferences and Writing,* Classics of Western Spirituality (Mahwah, NJ: Paulist Press, 1995).

Overall, the nineteenth century saw a significant development of new active women's communities.

There were also notable developments within the churches of the Reformation. For example, the spiritual landscape of nineteenth-century England was marked by two major movements in the Church of England. These were the Evangelical revival, which fostered the Reformed element in the church, and the so-called Oxford Movement, which promoted the Catholic dimension of Anglicanism. Without going into great detail about the theological bases of the two movements, both reflect in different ways the Way of Practical Action. The Evangelical revival has sometimes been accused of lacking a sense of social engagement. However, it promoted moral responsibility as part of its emphasis on conversion to the way of Christ. Beyond missionary "action," some figures in the movement also undertook social action. For example, John Newton, a priest in the City of London, was a major supporter of the campaign to abolish slavery. Hannah More was a notable educationalist and also active among the poor. William Wilberforce, after his Evangelical conversion, became one of the most noted social reformers as well as the leading figure in the antislavery movement. Finally, the Earl of Shaftesbury, a notable parliamentarian, was also one of the greatest social reformers of the century.[17]

The second notable nineteenth-century group within the Church of England was known as the Oxford Movement. This led to the formation of an explicit Anglican Catholic tradition. Again, without going into details about its ethos, a number of supporters of the movement were concerned with fostering social improvements in the rapidly expanding industrial cities. The strongly incarnational spirituality of the Catholic movement gave rise to a notable tradition of social theology and spirituality. This had theoretical aspects but was also actively expressed by the so-called slum priests in the East End of London. One example is Stewart Headlam, who founded the Guild of St. Matthew in 1877 to promote the study of social and political questions in the light of Christian doctrine. Ultimately, Headlam's Christian socialism led him into an active political life. Another

---

[17] See Ian Randall, *What a Friend We Have in Jesus: The Evangelical Tradition*, London: Darton, Longman & Todd, 2005.

important figure was Charles Gore, an academic theologian at Oxford, the first superior of the Community of the Resurrection (Mirfield Fathers), and eventually a diocesan bishop, who helped found the Christian Social Union.[18]

In the post–Civil War United States, two significant figures within mainstream Protestantism who followed the Way of Practical Action were the Baptist pastor Walter Rauschenbusch and Dana Webster Bartlett, a Congregationalist pastor. Rauschenbusch, one of best-known figures of the social gospel movement, worked among the poor of New York in the late nineteenth century. He held together classic evangelical revivalism and social concern. He anticipated twentieth-century spiritualities of liberation by asserting that true social change could be attained only if nourished by a deep spirituality. His deep commitment to spirituality led him to found the Little Society of Jesus in 1887 with two friends, Leighton Williams and Nathaniel Schmidt, who sought to emulate the Jesuits in some ways. The aim was a Jesus-centered spirituality combining Protestant and Catholic elements. The Little Society, later the Brotherhood of the Kingdom, had both social and spiritual values.[19]

There was also a Christian-inspired quest for more beautiful and healthier cities to counteract the crowded slums and belching factories.[20] One activist was the pastor Dana Webster Bartlett, who had ministered in the tenements of St. Louis, Missouri, and became one of the founders of the City Beautiful movement. He went to work in Los Angeles at the beginning of the twentieth century and promoted a movement of factories away from city centers to the edges and a move of working-class people from tenements to family homes with gardens. All this was intended to enhance the identities and lives of urban people. The downside was the birth of suburbia and therefore of urban sprawl.[21]

[18] See Geoffrey Rowell, Kenneth Stevenson, and Rowan Williams, eds., *Love's Redeeming Work: The Anglican Quest for Holiness* (Oxford: Oxford University Press, 2001), part 3.

[19] See Winthrop S. Hudson, ed., *Walter Rauschenbusch: Selected Writings*, Classics of Western Spirituality (Mahwah, NJ: Paulist Press), 1984.

[20] Joel Kotkin, *The City: A Global History* (New York: Random House, 2006), chapters 14 and 15.

[21] Dana Webster Bartlett, *The Better City: A Sociological Study of a Modern City* (Los Angeles: Neuner Company Press, 1907).

Twentieth Century

Turning to the twentieth century, much of the emphasis in spirituality expanded beyond a straightforward Way of Practical Action to embrace a more radical liberationist perspective. This will be explored more fully in chapter 6, which addresses the Prophetic Way.

In terms of the Way of Practical Action, there are a number of outstanding examples. Charles de Foucauld (1858–1916) and the new spiritual movement that he inspired are a good starting point. Although de Foucauld bridged the nineteenth and twentieth centuries, it was in the period after 1901 that he made his main spiritual impact. After life as a soldier and then an explorer in North Africa, de Foucauld underwent a religious conversion. He was ordained in France and then moved back to North Africa in 1901. He settled first at Beni Abbes and subsequently moved to Tamanrasett in southern Algeria, where he lived among the Tuareg people. He did not seek to convert them but learned their language, studied their culture, and lived a solitary, contemplative life among them. De Foucauld also had a counter-colonial desire to serve these people's needs. Sadly, he was killed during an uprising against the French in 1916 before he was able to found a new kind of religious community. However, Frère Charles de Jésus, as de Foucauld came to be known, inspired a new spiritual movement embodied in the Little Brothers and Sisters of Jesus. These live in small, semimonastic groups of four or five people, in ordinary apartments rather than in special buildings, in the poorest parts of Western cities and in regions of the developing world. The Little Brothers and Sisters do not undertake explicit social action but live in solidarity with those around them. They seek to be a contemplative and welcoming presence in the midst of their neighbors while supporting themselves in ordinary jobs alongside daily periods of prayer and silence.[22]

Then, second, there are the important writings of Evelyn Underhill. While Underhill's work is mainly associated with mysticism, she touches upon a number of other important aspects of Christian spirituality. For example, she had considerable sympathy for socialism

---

[22] See Robert Ellsberg, ed., *Charles de Foucauld: Selected Writings* (Maryknoll, NY: Orbis Books, 1999).

and maintained a strong sense of the social and ethical dimensions of spirituality. Underhill's most substantial book was *Mysticism*, which went through several editions and changes of perspective during her lifetime. Underhill's 1921 Upton Lectures, published the next year as *The Life of the Spirit and the Life of Today*, expressed a sense that inward transformation and outward action should be integrated in a more complete spirituality. Growth in spirituality no longer implies stepping aside from the everyday world; rather, it is a different way of being and acting in the world. By the 1930s Underhill had an overt interest in the relationship between mysticism and social awareness. However, conversely, while Underhill suggested that the particular genius of Christian spirituality was its link with action in the world, she also affirmed that social action without a spiritual dimension resulted in ethics without depth.[23]

Another important woman who pursued the Way of Practical Action was Dorothy Day (1897–1980). Day was one of the most influential figures in promoting a spirituality of social justice. After work as a labor activist and journalist, Dorothy Day became religious and explicitly a Roman Catholic. She found that the teachings of Christianity about disinterested love pointed toward a better way of responding to social issues. Through the French philosopher Pierre Maurin, who became her spiritual mentor, she came to identify closely with the poor. Together Day and Maurin founded the Catholic Worker Movement in New York in 1933 during the Great Depression.

The basis of Catholic Worker spirituality offered an alternative to secular socialism. Indeed, for Dorothy Day, there could be no authentic Christian spirituality that did not have attention to social issues as its core. The active spirituality of the movement is expressed particularly in houses of hospitality that offer a haven for marginalized people. These houses of hospitality currently number around a hundred and fifty across the United States, mostly in poor urban areas, although some are in rural farming communities. The basis for social spirituality is the Eucharist and common prayer. The Catholic Worker Movement is entirely lay and not only serves the poor but also undertakes direct action against social injustice. Although Dorothy Day

[23] See Underhill, *Mysticism*.

was a controversial figure because of her pacifism and acts of civil disobedience, by the time she died in 1980 she was widely admired. More recently her canonization has been promoted.[24]

While the Cistercian monk Thomas Merton (1915–1968), one of the greatest Roman Catholic spiritual writers of the twentieth century, is closely associated with monastic and contemplative spirituality, he was also a notable exponent of the Way of Practical Action. While remaining a monk of Gethsemani Abbey in Kentucky until his accidental death during an interfaith dialogue visit to Thailand in 1968, Merton also became famous for his later commitment to issues of social justice and world peace. Merton remained committed to his original option for a countercultural lifestyle but reinterpreted this in terms of his growing conviction that, in the face of a prevailing individualistic culture, the "true self" exists only in solidarity with what is "other." The authentic self is to be vulnerable rather than protected behind walls of separation and spiritual superiority. This growing insight led to a second conversion experience in the city near his monastery, Louisville, in the early 1960s. He was overwhelmed by a realization of his unity with and love for all the people on the sidewalks. This led him to a quite different sense of relationship to "the world": "It was like waking from a dream of separateness, of spurious self-isolation in a special world, the world of renunciation and supposed holiness. The whole illusion of a separate holy existence is a dream. . . . This sense of liberation from an illusory difference [between monastic life and ordinary people] was such a relief and such a joy to me that I almost laughed aloud."[25]

The corollary of this reconversion was a strong sense (expressed in his *Life and Holiness* of 1964) that the spiritual life is a matter not of quiet withdrawal but of awareness of our common responsibility for the future of humankind.[26]

---

[24] See Robert Ellsberg, ed., *Dorothy Day: Selected Writings* (Maryknoll, NY: Orbis Books, 1992).

[25] Merton, *Conjectures of a Guilty Bystander*, 140–41.

[26] See Lawrence S. Cunningham, ed., *Thomas Merton: Spiritual Master. The Essential Writings* (Mahwah, NJ: Paulist Press, 1992).

Conclusion: Ignatian Spirituality—Paradigm of the Way of Practical Action

As noted earlier, Ignatius Loyola, his famous *Spiritual Exercises*, and Ignatian spirituality more broadly are an important paradigm of the Way of Practical Action. Iñigo Lopez de Loyola was a Basque noble who initially followed a military and courtly career. He was wounded at the siege of Pamplona (1521) and subsequently underwent a religious conversion while recovering at his family castle. He then lived as a hermit at Manresa near Barcelona (1522–1523), where he received spiritual guidance at the monastery of Montserrat and learned the lessons of discernment as he slowly outgrew a tendency to excessive asceticism. The framework for his influential *Spiritual Exercises* was probably recorded at this time and further refined by subsequently guiding others. After a visit to the Holy Land, Ignatius undertook spiritual ministry as a layperson, returned to education at the universities of Alcalá and Salamanca, and gathered women and men followers. After being investigated by the Inquisition, he went to the University of Paris to study theology (1528–1535) and gathered another group of companions who eventually decided to be ordained and form a new religious community in order to effectively promote their spiritual ideals. Ignatius and his companions moved to Rome, where Ignatius obtained papal approval for the new order in 1540. The text of the *Spiritual Exercises* was approved in 1548 as a medium for spiritual formation. Ignatius remained in Rome as Jesuit Superior and died in 1556.

Ignatius's own spiritual experience and his work of guiding others are the key to the development of the *Spiritual Exercises* and Ignatian spirituality. Other influences were Jacopo de Voragine's lives of the saints and Ludolph of Saxony's *Life of Christ*—a text favored by the Devotio Moderna that suggested a form of imaginative gospel contemplation that was further developed in the *Exercises*.[27]

Apart from the famous and still widely used *Spiritual Exercises*, the body of writing associated with Ignatius includes *The Constitutions of the Society of Jesus*; his *Spiritual Diary*, which includes records of mystical illuminations; his so-called Autobiography, a dictated work

---

[27] On the influences on Ignatius, see Javier Melloni, *The Exercises of St. Ignatius Loyola in the Western Tradition* (Leominster, UK: Gracewing, 2000).

that runs up to 1538; and thousands of extant letters addressed to a wide range of people, many of them focused on spiritual guidance. These are a rich source of insight into his spiritual wisdom.[28]

The *Spiritual Exercises* is one of the most influential spiritual texts of all time and is nowadays used as a medium for spiritual guidance across an ecumenical spectrum of Christians. The text is not meant to be inspirational but is instead a series of practical notes for retreat guides to help them to facilitate a spiritual transformation process adjusted to the needs of each person making the retreat. The norm is a month away from everyday responsibilities, but a modified form "in the midst of daily life" is also outlined.

Much of the text consists of advice about the structure and content of prayer (five periods a day in the full version), guidance about spiritual discernment and making a choice of life, and helpful suggestions about practical matters such as the physical environment for prayer, the use of penance, and rules about eating and handling scruples.

The explicit aim of the *Spiritual Exercises* is to assist people in being freed from disordered attachments, growing in spiritual freedom, and responding to the call of Christ to join him in mission. There are four phases, called "Weeks," each with a specific focus, that enable this process to unfold. The originality of the text lies not in the content or methods of prayer but in the structure and dynamic. The First Week begins with human sinfulness, but in the context of a growing awareness of God's unwavering love. We are to recognize that sinfulness is no bar to responding to God's call. The Second Week deepens the sense of being called to "be with" Christ in mission, developed through a series of contemplations on the life and work of Christ. This gradually leads the retreatant to face a choice (or "Election") highlighted by three meditations on the contrasting values of Christ and the world. This leads the retreatant to consider the cost of following Christ—expressed in the Third Week meditations on Christ's suffering and death. This leads the retreatant during the Fourth Week

---

[28] The texts of the Autobiography, *Spiritual Diary*, and *Spiritual Exercises*, plus selections of letters, are available in Joseph Munitiz and Philip Endean eds., *Saint Ignatius of Loyola: Personal Writings* (London: Penguin Books, 1996). An accessible recent study of Ignatian spirituality is David Lonsdale, *Eyes to See, Ears to Hear: An Introduction to Ignatian Spirituality* (London: Darton, Longman & Todd, 2000).

to experience something of the joy and hope of Christ's resurrection. The *Exercises* ends with the "Contemplation on the Love of God," which acts as a bridge back into everyday life, now transformed into a context for finding the presence of God in all things.

From the *Exercises*, it is possible to detect fundamental features of Ignatian spirituality. First, God is encountered particularly in everyday life, which itself becomes a "spiritual exercise." Second, the life and death of Jesus Christ is the fundamental pattern for Christian life. Third, God revealed in Christ offers healing, liberation, and hope. Fourth, spirituality involves a deepening desire for God (our "desire" is a key idea in the text) and the experience of God's acceptance in return. The final theme of "finding God in all things" promotes the integration of contemplation and action. The idea of following the pattern of Christ focuses on actively sharing in God's mission to the world—not least responding to people in need.

Finally, at the heart of our spiritual process lies the gift of discernment—an increasing ability to judge wisely and to choose well in ways that are congruent with each person's deepest truth. In Ignatian spirituality, discernment implies the wisdom to recognize the difference between courses of action that are life-directing and ones that are out of harmony with our relationship with God. Faced with choices, we are subject to contradictory influences. Some of these incline us to what is life-giving (what Ignatius calls "consolation") and others to what is flawed (what he calls "desolation"). As Ignatius recognized, desire is what powers our spiritualities. For each person, certain desires have the potential to shape serious choices and therefore to give direction to our lives. Discernment enables us to be aware of the full range of desires that we experience. In terms of the Way of Practical Action, discernment is a critical value when it comes to decisions about how to exist in society and how best to act in the world.

Both discernment and the process of becoming free from our unhelpful dependencies, or "disordered attachments," demand a contemplative attentiveness. Ignatian spirituality has promoted a range of spiritual practices and approaches to prayer and contemplation both within the *Exercises* and in the large collection of Ignatius's letters. No single method can be uniquely described as "Ignatian prayer." There are at least ten mentioned in the *Exercises*, many of them originating in the Devotio Moderna tradition and, more remotely, in adaptations of monastic *lectio divina*. Three methods are particularly striking in terms of cultivating attentiveness and discernment. The first, gospel contemplation, offers a structured approach to scriptural meditation via the use of imagination as we seek to enter into a gospel scene. This process of "being present" is not aimed at pious satisfaction but, through intimate association with what is portrayed in Scripture, lays us open to challenge and to the risk of being profoundly changed. The second method, the daily Examen, outlines a brief practice of reflection on our experience of each day—noting where God was active and where we have responded to or failed to respond to God's action. Finally, in an appendix to the *Exercises* entitled "Three Ways of Prayer," there is the "prayer of the breath." This suggests the slow, rhythmic, recitation of a familiar prayer, such as the Our Father, with each word linked to our rhythmic breathing. This approach is close to Eastern Christian hesychastic practices or to meditation in the Al-Andalus Sufi tradition that would have been known in late-medieval Spain. Again, such prayer is not merely a matter of achieving peace and stillness but also enables a deep process of engagement with God and therefore of transformation.

Precisely because Ignatian spirituality emphasizes practical everyday action, the *Spiritual Exercises* also encourages a strongly contemplative attitude—summarized in the distinctive ideas of becoming a "contemplative in action" and of the growing capacity to "find God in all things." Indeed, Ignatius himself manifested in his life and practice what may be called a "mysticism of service."

CHAPTER FIVE

The Way of Beauty

The Way of Beauty is perhaps less familiar than other types of Christian spirituality. Classic studies of Christian spirituality have tended to concentrate on more obviously spiritual or mystical writings, the stories of key personalities, or the history of important movements such as monasticism. However, nature and landscapes, the arts, music, and poetry also offer rich possibilities for the spiritual way.

For example, the Way of Beauty, expressed in the arts and the relationship between the arts and spirituality, has a long history in Europe. While in late modernity spirituality appeared to disappear as an explicit theme in art, the great twentieth-century German theologian Karl Rahner nevertheless argued that genuinely spiritual art appeared beyond the boundaries of organized religion. For example, he spoke of the "anonymous reverence" of French Impressionist paintings.[1] Art has a capacity to evoke reverence, to awaken the depths of human experience, and constantly to provoke the transgression of material boundaries. The important point is that the Way of Beauty takes us beyond conventional written texts to include nature, the creative arts, music, architecture, and literature, especially poetry.[2]

---

[1] See Karl Rahner, "Art against the Horizon of Theology and Piety," in his *Theological Investigations*, vol. 23 (London: Darton, Longman & Todd, 1992), 162–68, especially 167.

[2] See David Tracy, *On Naming the Present: God, Hermeneutics and Church* (Maryknoll, NY: Orbis Books, 1994), 115–18.

Spiritual Experience and Nature

I want to begin my reflections on the Way of Beauty with the potential of nature, especially landscapes, to evoke the spiritual and to provoke a deepening of the human spirit. As noted in chapter 3, Christian mystical literature has frequently used natural imagery—for example, mountains in Gregory of Nyssa or John of the Cross. While for many people landscape can simply be a backdrop, for others it can become an organic part of life. We all have preferred landscapes. For some people it is wild nature, for others it is the forest, and for many it is hills and mountains.

In my own case, I grew up near a beautiful forest inhabited by wild ponies and deer, while on the other side of town there was an undulating landscape saturated with history in the remains of Bronze Age settlements, Celtic burial mounds, Roman hill forts, and medieval castles and field systems. But more than anything else, the sea was a powerful and evocative force. As a child I always lived close to the ocean and went to a school that overlooked cliffs and beaches. Although as children we were taught that wild waves could be dangerous, we also learned to trust ourselves to the sea as we swam or floated on the water while gazing up at the vast sky.

> Delightful I think it to be in the bosom of an isle, on the peak of a rock, that I might often see there the calm of the sea.
>
> That I might see its heavy waves over the glittering ocean, as they chant a melody to their Father on their eternal course.[3]

These words from an ancient Celtic Christian source beautifully capture my experience of the constantly changing nature of the sea, whether flat calm or heavy waves, with the effect of light on water and the sound of the tide advancing on shingled beaches.[4]

---

[3] K. Hurlstone Jackson, ed., *A Celtic Miscellany: Translations from the Celtic Literature* (London: Penguin Classics, 1971), no. 222, p. 279.

[4] On spirituality and landscape, see, for example, Belden Lane, *The Solace of Fierce Landscapes: Exploring Desert and Mountain Spirituality* (New York: Oxford University Press, 1998). See also Sheldrake, *Living Between Worlds*, chapter 2, "Landscape and Sacred Sites," and chapter 6, "The Natural World"; and Philip Sheldrake, *Spaces for the Sacred: Place Memory and Identity* (London: SCM Press, 2001), chapter 1, "A Sense of Place."

Aesthetics and Spirituality

Turning now to the arts, at their heart is the power of human imagination. This is particularly prominent in some religious traditions. For example, there is a strongly aesthetic dimension at the heart of Eastern Orthodox spirituality. This is best known through the tradition of icons. A famous example is the fifteenth-century icon of the Trinity by Andrei Rublev, considered to be one of the greatest achievements of Russian art. Importantly, icons are understood to be more than mere works of art. They are seen as channels of God's power. There is a quasi-mystical understanding that through our interaction with icons we may become united with what the icon represents: the Trinity, Christ, the Virgin Mary, or saints.

In nonreligious contexts, aesthetics has become an important medium of contemporary spirituality. The word *aesthetics* comes from the Greek *aisthetikos*, "concerning perception," meaning how we come to understand reality through our senses. Major philosophers from Immanuel Kant to Martin Heidegger wrote in various ways about "beauty." For some, this concept is not merely concerned with what is attractive but is connected with the sublime—that is, what relates to the sacred, to the quest for ultimate meaning, and to integrity. At the heart of all the arts is the power of the image. That is, the artist creates an image and communicates via imagery, and the audience receives "meaning" through imagination. In other words, musical, artistic, and literary images have a capacity to touch the spiritual depths of human experience beyond the limits of rational language and physical observation.

Historically, the creative arts in Western culture have deep religious roots. For example, there is an obvious religious depth in the art of Michelangelo, in the poetry of George Herbert, or in the music of Johann Sebastian Bach. Equally, all religions use artistic forms of various kinds. There is a riot of painting and sculpture in Hindu temples, the cosmic architecture of the great medieval cathedrals, the chanting of Buddhist monks, and the music and poetry of Sufi Islam. Outside religion, some Western artists approach their work as both a philosophy of life and a form of spiritual practice. In Vincent Van Gogh, art expressed a great longing "like a light in the midst of darkness." The artist Wassily Kandinsky was influenced by Rudolph

Steiner and anthroposophy. He suggested that "to send light into the darkness of men's hearts—such is the duty of the artist." Another twentieth-century artist, Piet Mondrian, believed that an artist was able to attain ideal art only by reaching a point where there was direct and conscious interaction with the spiritual. More widely, for many people aesthetic experience is an intense source of self-transcendence.

Music also plays a role in all the major world religions. While it often accompanies the performance of religious ritual, it is sometimes also considered to be a spiritual expression in itself. Some religious music has an enthusiastic following among nonreligious people. An interesting example is the ethereal and evocative sound of Gregorian plainchant, particularly when sung by monastic communities. Numerous excellent contemporary recordings are available, especially from French monasteries such as Solesmes, St. Wandrille, Ligugé, and En-Calcat.

A number of twentieth-century classical composers also engaged overtly with the spiritual. For example, German composer Paul Hindemith and French composer Olivier Messiaen in their different ways suggested that sound in itself was symbolic of the spiritual because it connects us to the universal harmonies of the cosmos. Arnold Schoenberg, in his opera *Moses und Aaron* and through his contrast between sensuality and silence, portrayed his understanding of the fundamental spiritual conflict of the twentieth century. American composer John Cage based his highly abstract work on his study of Buddhist philosophy. In a very different mode, Estonian minimalist composer Arvo Pärt is inspired partly by Western monastic chant and partly by the liturgy of the Orthodox Church.

It is also noticeable that spiritual experience has had an impact on elements of European musical theater in recent decades. This approach to theater emphasizes its role as the enactment and embodiment of meaning. For example, MusikTheaterKöln has been using mystical texts, both Buddhist and Christian, since the mid-1990s. Thus, Zen koans from the Mumonkan have been the basis for musical theater. The chamber opera *Las Canciones* was based on the poetry of the sixteenth-century Spanish mystic John of the Cross and sought, through text and music, to express the surrender of the human soul to God.

Finally, in a broad-based collection of essays, *Art and the Spiritual*, such major artists and film directors as Antony Gormley, Bill Viola, and David Puttnam engaged with key themes at the interface of the arts and the spiritual.[5] These include the importance of the accidental and surprising; the experience of "the angelic" (that is, spiritual powers that are both revealing and challenging); art as a liminal-transitional place; and stained glass as a way of mediating the outside and inside. All of the contributors agree that the power of art-as-spiritual is that while art arises out of an engagement with the everyday material world, at the same time it offers a spiritual sense of the wholeness of humanity and transforms how we see the world.

In the remainder of this chapter I will briefly explore the aesthetics of the Impressionist movement of art and music and then outline the spiritual qualities of medieval religious architecture. Finally, I will look at religious poetry, taking the great seventeenth-century poet George Herbert as my example.

The Aesthetics of Impressionism

An ambiguous example of spiritual vision in relation to aesthetics is the artistic movement known as Impressionism, which, as already noted, Rahner associated with "anonymous reverence." The concept of Impressionism embraces European painting and music and began in the second half of the nineteenth century. Beyond its particular techniques lay a theory and a philosophy. This theory attempted to portray a different way of seeing that broke through the conventional boundaries, not least of what we understand by "beauty."

The emphasis in Impressionist painting was on immediacy and spontaneity; on the depiction of light, particularly its changing qualities; on movement as crucial to human experience and perception; on unusual visual angles; and on outdoor painting rather than work in studios. Outdoor work enabled the artist to capture the momentary and transient play of light, including shadows. Equally, nature was not the object of exact representation but allowed for subjective perception. The theory behind Impressionism was a search for beauty

---

[5] Bill Hall and David Jasper, eds., *Art and the Spiritual* (Sunderland, UK: University of Sunderland Press, 2003).

as "the real" versus perfect, idealized forms. There was also a search for the ephemeral and the transient as opposed to fixed formalities. An important earlier artist who inspired the Impressionists was the great English romantic painter J. M. W. Turner. Among the best-known Impressionist painters were Claude Monet, Pierre-Auguste Renoir, Alfred Sisley, Edgar Degas, Edouard Manet, Camille Pissaro, and Paul Cézanne.

The movement known as Impressionism also produced a distinctive approach to classical music in the late nineteenth and early twentieth centuries. This music sought to convey mood and emotion (but not emotional excess) as opposed to a detailed tone picture. The idea or effect that composers sought to communicate was through what might be called a wash of sound rather than a strict formal structure. Again, in ways parallel to Impressionist painting, the music was somewhat dematerialized, shimmering and vibrating. There was also a certain ambiguity or understatement. There were provocatively colorful effects created through orchestration, new chord combinations, extended harmonies, and ambiguous tonality. Equally, there was a somewhat unresolved quality in Impressionist music in which the evocation of mood, feeling, and atmosphere had priority. Overall, the aim of Impressionist music was to convey the notion that pure sound was a beautiful and mysterious end in itself.

Some of the best-known exponents within a broad interpretation of Impressionist music were French composers Claude Debussy and Maurice Ravel, Spaniards Manuel de Falla and Isaac Albeniz, Italian Ottorino Respighi, and English composers Ralph Vaughan-Williams (a student of Ravel), John Ireland, and Frederick Delius. Some commentators also associate Erik Satie and Jean Sibelius with Impressionist music.

It is sometimes said that Impressionist music has a distinctive spiritual quality. Yet many of its exponents were not conventionally religious. For example, Ravel was an atheist, Vaughan-Williams was an agnostic, and Delius's *Mass of Life* and *Requiem* were pantheistic rather than conventionally Christian. That said, the spiritual quality of Impressionism, whether in art or in music, is expressed in several ways. For example, in painting, the preference for the outdoors brings the artist closer to nature (creation). The emphasis on feelings includes touching serenity and peace. In art there is a clear emphasis on being present, and in this experience of presence beauty can be found in the ordinary, not least in the particularity of place. Equally, Impressionism suggests that all human experiences are "impressions" that point beyond the immediate to the "more" and "greater." Also, every such impression, while in some sense incomplete, is nevertheless unique. Finally, Impressionism, in both art and music, draws in the observer or listener to become a participant rather than a detached observer.

Medieval Religious Architecture— The Great Gothic Churches

My next example of the Way of Beauty is medieval religious architecture, specifically the Gothic style. This is an artistic form with powerful spiritual resonances. One striking example of the spiritual power of such religious buildings is people's continued fascination with the great medieval cathedrals of Western Europe, even in a supposedly post-religious age. Such buildings continue to attract large numbers of visitors who seek something more than the mere chance to visit a museum or a historic monument.

The original theory behind medieval Gothic church architecture was overtly spiritual. In these buildings, paradise was evoked and expressed in material terms through the design, the layout, and the artwork. To enter a great church was to be transported into a transcendent realm by the space, light, color, and architecture. The architecture of medieval cathedrals acted as a microcosm of the universe and sought to express a peaceable oneness between Creator and creation. This was a utopian space in which an idealized cosmic harmony was portrayed in the material everyday world.

For medieval people to enter such a building was to be transported into a vision of heaven on earth by the juxtaposition of vast and intimate spaces and by the progressive dematerialization of walls into a sea of glass and a flood of light. During the twelfth century, Abbot Suger of St. Denis in Paris was one of the greatest patrons and theorists of early Gothic. For Suger, a church building had to be more impressive than other city buildings precisely because it stood for a transcendent vision.

At their best, the great medieval churches promoted more than a two-dimensional, static "map" of the surrounding city. They also portrayed another dimension of human existence—movement through space from earth to heaven, plus a journey of human transformation through the process of time. For example, Norwich Cathedral in England has a cycle of 250 medieval roof bosses. These run down the center of the cathedral roof vaulting from the part of the building known as the choir back through the nave to end at the west door. The bosses portray a biblical history of salvation beginning with the Fall and ending with the ascension, final judgment, and heaven. It is significant that the Fall is nearest to the high altar and the final judgment and paradise are nearest to the west door. As a visual pilgrimage, it moves from the most obviously sacred part of the cathedral to the exit back into the city streets. It is not too far-fetched to suggest that this implicitly represents the viewpoint of the wealthy Norwich merchant class that undoubtedly helped the Benedictine monks who ran the cathedral to fund much of the cathedral decoration. The direction of the visual journey back to the main entrance and exit suggests that the city itself should be understood as a sacred place.

Interestingly, a famous feature of the great French Gothic Chartres Cathedral has captured the imagination of people who are not conventionally religious. This is the labyrinth etched on the floor of its nave and originally intended to be a microcosm both of the physical pilgrimage to Jerusalem for those who did not have the means to undertake it and of the pilgrimage through human life to our eternal destiny. Versions of this labyrinth design appeared in other medieval cathedrals, either in a form that enabled walking meditation or, as at Lucca in Italy, as a miniature on the wall outside the cathedral entrance. A pilgrim would presumably trace the design with a finger before entering the sacred space. The walking labyrinth of Chartres is nowadays reproduced around the world, not just in centers of spirituality but also in parks and city squares. To walk the labyrinth cultivates attentiveness, persistence, and stillness and also symbolizes the quest for ultimate enlightenment. Because there are no false avenues or dead ends in a labyrinth (as opposed to a maze), the conclusion of the walking meditation is always to arrive at the center.

Sacred space is also deeply connected to memory. For example, the great medieval cathedrals are repositories for the cumulative memory and constantly renewed hopes of the local city community. Such churches are what may be called a "memory palace"—that is, a constant reminder that memory in itself is vital to a healthy sense of identity, both individually and collectively. This is expressed structurally in civic and other public monuments, in chantry chapels commemorating the local gentry, in the tombs of holy people, and more subtly through an intangible atmosphere resulting from generations of pilgrims and visitors. Even today, to enter such a building is to engage with centuries of human pain, achievement, hopes, and ideals. American philosopher Arnold Berleant suggests that the great urban cathedrals also acted—and may still act—as guides to what he calls an "urban ecology" that contrasts with the monotony of the modern city, "thus helping transform it from a place where one's humanity is constantly threatened into a place where it is continually achieved and enlarged."[6] Cathedrals may still be effective centers in our contemporary cities. Such urban buildings offer communion with something deeper than our need for an ordered public life or efficient city systems. Cathedrals deliberately speak of the condition of the world.

It is now widely recognized that there was a diversity of aesthetics and concepts of beauty, and therefore of theological symbolism, during the age of medieval Gothic architecture. This has been emphasized in an illuminating study of medieval art and concepts of beauty by Umberto Eco.[7] Gothic space has been characterized as, among other things, dematerialized and spiritualized. It thereby expressed the limitless quality of an infinite God through the soaring verticality of arches and vaults. These were a deliberate antithesis to human scale. Nor can the medieval fascination with the symbolism of numbers be ignored. The basic three-story elevation of Gothic church architecture (that is, the main arcade, the triforium, and the clerestory) cannot be explained merely by advances in engineering. Both Rupert of Deutz and Abbot Suger in the twelfth century drew explicit attention to the trinitarian symbolism of this three-story elevation. However, later Gothic buildings, such as the world-famous King's College Chapel in Cambridge, are notable for another feature that was typical

---

[6] Arnold Berleant, *The Aesthetics of Environment* (Philadelphia: Temple University Press, 1992), 62.

[7] Umberto Eco, *Art and Beauty in the Middle Ages* (New Haven, CT: Yale University Press, 1986).

of their period. The stone walls that support King's College Chapel have been reduced to a minimum and replaced by vast expanses of glass. The biblical stories portrayed in the stained glass of the windows taught worshipers a great deal about the Christian doctrine of God, creation, and salvation. However, there was also a sense in which colored glass and its patterned effect on the stonework of the interior of the building expressed what has been called "a metaphysics of light." God was increasingly proclaimed as both the one who dwelled in inaccessible light and the one whose divine light illuminated the world.[8]

Until recently there has been an unbalanced concentration on a metaphysics of light derived from the anonymous late-fifth-century Eastern Christian mystical theologian Pseudo-Dionysius. In fact, it is now considered that St. Augustine's aesthetics played at least as important a part in the monastic theology of someone such as Abbot Suger as did the theology of Pseudo-Dionysius. Indeed, in medieval thought and design the Dionysian elements are often intermingled with Augustine's thought.[9] Hence the concept of *harmonia*—that is, a fitting order or beauty—established by God is a central theme. This refers both to the building and to the worshiping community that it houses. Abbot Suger referred to "perspicacious order" as the key to his vision for the Abbey of Saint-Denis and for other Gothic churches, and in Augustine *ordo* is the characteristic word in reference to the harmonious beauty of the cosmos.[10]

This mixture of Augustinian and Dionysian elements has led to contemporary rereadings of Suger's thinking when he reconstructed the Abbey of Saint-Denis, a building considered central to the development of subsequent Gothic churches. Suger is full of Augustine's

---

[8] For some reflections on what might be called the theology of Gothic, see Christopher Wilson, *The Gothic Cathedral* (London: Thames and Hudson, 1990), especially the introduction, 64–66, 219–20, 262–63.

[9] On this mixture of theological aesthetics, see the essay by Bernard McGinn, "From Admirable Tabernacle to the House of God: Some Theological Reflections on Medieval Architectural Integration," in Virginia Chieffo Raguin, Kathryn Brush, and Peter Draper, eds., *Artistic Integration in Gothic Buildings* (Toronto: University of Toronto Press, 1995).

[10] *Libellus Alter De Consecratione Ecclesiae Sancti Dionysii*, IV, translated in Erwin Panofsky, *Abbot Suger on the Abbey Church of St. Denis and Its Art Treasures*, 2nd ed. (Princeton, NJ: Princeton University Press, 1979), 100–1.

sense of *harmonia* as order and beauty. For Suger, the inner meaning of a theory of signs always pointed beyond the external material order to what was "more," "greater," or "higher." Beyond the aesthetic of the physical beauty of a building lay a higher sense of beauty that provoked a transition from the material world to the spiritual realm. Abbot Suger actually quoted Augustine in the original Latin inscription on his new, great west doors of the abbey church.

> Whoever you are, if you seek to extol the glory of these doors
> Do not marvel at the gold and the expense but at the craftsmanship
>   of the work.
> Bright is the noble work; but, being nobly bright, the work
> Should brighten the minds so that they may travel through the true
>   lights . . .
> To the true light where Christ is the true door.
> The gold door defines the manner in which it is inherent.
> The dull mind rises to truth through what is material
> And, in seeing this light, is resurrected from its former submersion.

The implication was that a higher understanding would see the physical door of the church as the "door of Paradise." Abbot Suger summarized here his theology both of light and of the great building as a symbol of paradise.

An Augustinian approach to understanding the integration of architectural style and buildings would certainly involve a fundamental understanding of the church as a community of people—the faithful who make up the Body of Christ. This is the *tabernaculum admirabile,* the "wonderful tabernacle," as explained in Augustine's sermon on Psalm 41 (in the Vulgate), within which one attains to God.[11]

However, this *tabernaculum admirabile* of the Christian community also needs a *locus,* that is, a physical place where the community is both shown forth and continually reinforced. This "place" is first of all the church's liturgy and secondly the building that contains this action. Part of what lay behind Abbot Suger's "reading" of a church

---

[11] Philip Schaff, ed., *A Select Library of the Nicene and Post-Nicene Fathers of The Christian Church* (Grand Rapids, MI: Eerdmans, 1996), vol. 8, St. Augustine, "Expositions on the Book of Psalms," Psalm 42, section 8, 134.

building was sacramental theology. To house the Christian liturgy was not merely a mechanical or practical issue—for example, developing passageways for processions or placing windows so as to provide light for critical liturgical focuses at the high altar.[12] A key feature of the theology of Abbot Suger and of medieval churches is that the material realm is not incidental, but necessary in order to draw humanity upward to the heavenly realm. In the mind of someone such as Abbot Suger, a church building should not only be adequate for public worship but should also evoke wonder and point beyond itself to the eternal dwelling place of God. In this way of seeing things, the church building is a doorway or access point. Its harmony is represented not simply by geometry, architectural coherence, or artwork but also by the degree to which it fulfills this function of access. That is the beauty, the *harmonia*, of a religious building such as a Gothic cathedral.

It is also important to add that medieval people had an integrated worldview rather than a differentiated one. They conceived of an ultimate unity in the universe. The conception of the Gothic cathedral is a good example. Each detail in the building recapitulates the overall architectonic design of the structure as a whole. However, this equally reflects in stone a theological and spiritual approach to human life in which the whole is somehow reflected in each part.

Every element of the building could be interpreted in reference to a higher meaning. "Those who criticise us claim that the sacred function needs only a holy soul and a pure mind. We certainly agree that these are what principally matter, but we believe also that we should worship through the outward ornaments of sacred vessels . . . and this with all inner purity and with all outward splendour."[13]

Alongside Augustine's theology, both Abbot Suger and the Abbey of Saint-Denis were inevitably influenced by the thought of Pseudo-Dionysius. For one thing, Pseudo-Dionysius was thought to be the same as the Saint Denis who was supposedly buried in the abbey church. The monastery also preserved the Greek text of Pseudo-Dionysius's *Theologia Mystica*. An important element of Dionysian

---

[12] On such practicalities and their impact on architectural developments, see Richard Morris, *Churches in the Landscape* (London: J. M. Dent, 1989), 96–98 and 289–95.
[13] *Libellus Alter De Consecratione Ecclesiae Sancti Dionysii*, IV.

theology is the concept of light. God can be spoken of especially as light. "Light comes from the Good, and light is an image of this archetypal Good. Thus the Good is also praised by the name 'Light', just as an archetype is revealed in its image. The goodness of the transcendent God reaches from the highest and most perfect forms of being to the very lowest. And yet it remains above and beyond them all, superior to the highest and yet stretching out to the lowliest. It gives light to everything capable of receiving it, it creates them, keeps them alive, preserves and perfects them."[14] Everything created stems from that initial uncreated light. The cosmos was a kind of explosion of light, and the divine light united everything, linking all things by love and with Love. There was, therefore, an overarching coherence. A gradual ascent or movement back toward the source of all things and all light complemented the outward movement of the divine into the cosmos. Everything returned by means of the visible, from the created to the uncreated.[15] The principal theme was the oneness of the universe. However, although we may describe God as Light, according to Pseudo-Dionysius's own principles (especially as taught in the *Theologia Mystica*), we must also deny that God can be defined as anything in particular. God is neither this, nor that—not even Supreme Light. Eternal reality is ultimately beyond our conception.

> Trinity! Higher than any being,
> Any divinity, any goodness!
> Guide of Christians
> In the wisdom of heaven!
> Lead us up beyond unknowing and light,
> Up to the farthest, highest peak
> Of mystic scripture,
> Where the mysteries of God's Word
> Lie simple, absolute and unchangeable
> In the brilliant darkness of a hidden silence.
> Amid the deepest shadow

---

[14] *The Divine Names* 4.4, in Luibheid and Rorem, *Pseudo-Dionysius*, 74.

[15] For a brief summary of Dionysian theory, see Sheldrake, *Spirituality and History*, 200–1. See also Georges Duby, *The Age of the Cathedral: Art and Society 980–1420* (Chicago: University of Chicago Press, 1981), 99–100.

They pour overwhelming light
On what is most manifest.
Amid the wholly unsensed and unseen
They completely fill our sightless minds
With treasures beyond all beauty.[16]

After Abbot Suger's time, Gothic architectural and artistic portray-
als of God also focused on the incarnation—the joining of God with
human nature. As a result, one of the greatest symbols of the doctrine
of the incarnation and of the humanity of Jesus, the Virgin Mary our
Mother, was situated at the heart of the iconography of cathedral
glass. Scenes of the annunciation, the visitation, and the nativity were
found on the decoration of high altars. The Christianity embodied in
Gothic architecture was built upon a theology of God as almighty
and unknowable, yet incarnate and revealed. Gothic church architecture portrayed humanity as graced with divine illumination.

It has been said of medieval visitors to cathedrals that "they were
the enraptured witnesses of a new way of seeing."[17] What is this new
way of seeing? For those who knew the codes, in a sense the cathedrals and other great medieval churches contained all the information
in the world and about the world. The new way of seeing derived
from visual and other material aids that drew the participant onward
from self-awareness to a deeper awareness of God as the focus of a
higher vision. The twelfth-century Parisian theologian Richard of
St. Victor described these modes of vision in his commentary on the
book of Revelation. There were four modes of vision, divided between the bodily and the spiritual. In the first, we open our eyes to
what is there—the color, the shapes, the harmony—a simple seeing
of material objects. In the second, we view the outward appearances
but also see beyond them to a deeper mystical significance. The movement is from immediate perception to a deeper knowledge. In the
third mode, we move to the first part of spiritual seeing. Here there
is a discovery of the truth of hidden things, such as the writer of the
book of Revelation himself experienced, according to Richard of

---

[16] *The Mystical Theology* 1.1, in Luibheid and Rorem, *Pseudo-Dionysius,* 135.
[17] Michael Camille, *Gothic Art: Visions and Revelations of the Medieval World* (London:
Weidenfeld & Nicolson, 1996), 12.

St. Victor. Finally, in the fourth mode of vision, we reach the deepest level of spiritual seeing. This is the mystical level. Here one has been drawn through the other modes to a pure and naked seeing of divine reality.

The "real" lay beyond the immediate realm of the senses. Abbot Suger understood the architecture of churches to be a harmonization of opposites—the act of divine creation reflected in the church building: "The awesome power of one sole and supreme Reason reconciles the disparity between all things of Heaven and Earth by due proportion: this same sweet concord, itself alone, unites what seem to oppose each other, because of their base origins and contrary natures, into a single exalted and well-tuned Harmony."[18]

In fact, the Christian theology of physical sacred places, such as great churches or other places of pilgrimage, is also essentially associated with people, living or dead, who acted as "places" of the sacred. Medieval pilgrimages led to the shrines of saints—for example, the supposed tomb of the Apostle James at Santiago de Compostela. The great churches were simply spaces within which the ongoing story of God's dealings with the human community could be told through architecture, glass, stone, and artwork. If the architectural order of the great churches was a microcosm of the cosmic order, that order consisted of a hierarchy of beings rather than simply an impersonal geometrical pattern.

In social terms, the development of the great medieval cathedrals was most obviously an urban phenomenon. It also represented an eschatological shift.[19] In the early Middle Ages, the dominant image of heaven was the recreation of a Garden of Eden—for example, in monastic settlements. After about 1150, the first major urban renewal since the death of the Western Roman Empire took place. This had a major impact on social and theological perspectives, even though cities still embraced only some 5 percent of the European population. In terms of biblical theology, there was a gradual move from the book of Genesis to the book of Revelation, from the restoration of the Garden of Eden to the New Jerusalem. At the heart of the new cities

---

[18] *Libellus Alter De Consecratione Ecclesiae Sancti Dionysii*, IV, 82.

[19] See Colleen McDannell and Bernhard Lang, *Heaven, A History* (New Haven, CT: Yale University Press, 1988), 70–80. See also Duby, *The Age of the Cathedral*, part 2.

there appeared the great cathedrals and the new Gothic style of architecture.

As a final remark, it has already been noted that the art of the medieval cathedrals sought to evoke a peaceable oneness between Creator and creation. This was a utopian space in which a heavenly harmony was anticipated in the here and now. However, to be realistic, in its historical context such harmony was *idealized*. As Georges Duby, the distinguished French medievalist, reminds us, "Yet it would be a mistake to assume that the Thirteenth Century wore the beaming face of the crowned Virgin or the smiling angels. The times were hard, tense, and very wild, and it is important that we recognise all that was tumultuous and rending about them."[20] The social symbolism of the great medieval cathedrals was thus also ambiguous. We cannot ignore the fact that while such cathedrals symbolized a Christian vision of human-divine unity, they also solidified the divisions of the prevailing social order. The Gothic cathedrals of the High Middle Ages sanctioned the new urban wealth from which they derived. They also proclaimed episcopal power and religious orthodoxy.

> Cathedrals also demarcated interior spaces; some parts were reserved for clergy alone, and in the laity's space, subdivisions reflected ranks and distinctions, and substantiated a hierarchical order with seats given over to the powerful who did not wish to stand and could afford particular proximity to the holy. Special chapels served select groups, and pictorial representations, by privileging certain groups and implicitly rejecting others, contributed to the cathedral's role in organising, enacting, and publicizing a hierarchy of social differentiation.[21]

Harmonia—order or beauty—tended to be conservative in its results. The perfect, harmonious community could not but reflect the social hierarchies and values of the times. For example, it has been noted that representations of heaven idealized in the art of medieval cathedrals

---

[20] Duby, *The Age of the Cathedral*, 95.
[21] Brigette Bedos-Rozak, "Form as Social Process," in Raguin, Brush, and Draper, *Artistic Integration in Gothic Buildings*, 243–44.

tended to reproduce rather than subvert the separation of laity from clergy and the peasantry from the aristocracy and the monarchy. Thus, in the words of Aloysius Pieris, the Sri Lankan Jesuit liberation theologian involved in interreligious dialogue, on the west front of Chartres Cathedral above the great door there are "elongated figures of 'saints' thinned out of the world to reach a God above, and stout, stocky figures of this-worldly artisans and peasants supporting with the sweat of their brows that other 'leisure class' who have all the time and energy for liturgies and mystical contemplation, point to a conception of spirituality indelibly sculptured in the cathedrals of our collective unconscious."[22]

Spirituality and Poetry: George Herbert

At the end of this chapter, and as a final paradigm of the Way of Beauty, I want to mention the power of poetry. In terms of literature, spirituality is most explicitly present in religious poets. Famous examples include the Persian Sufi Rumi, the Bengali Rabindranath Tagore, English seventeenth-century metaphysical poets such as John Donne and George Herbert, the nineteenth-century English Jesuit Gerard Manley Hopkins, and more recently the poetry of the late Elizabeth Jennings and the late R. S. Thomas. The example I will now examine briefly is the poetry of the great seventeenth-century poet and Anglican priest George Herbert (1593–1633).

The person and writings of George Herbert are a striking example of the Anglican spiritual tradition. Herbert was a member of the aristocratic and powerful Pembroke family. He led a varied life, first as a Fellow of Trinity College Cambridge and university orator, and then as a member of parliament, before finally being ordained and becoming a country parish priest in the Wiltshire village of Bemerton in1630. His two great works are the prose treatise on priestly life and ministry *The Country Parson* and the great poetic collection *The Temple*. Although *The Country Parson* deserves to be redeemed as a work of spiritual literature, there can be no doubt that the poems make the greater spiritual as well as aesthetic impact on the modern reader

---

[22] Aloysius Pieris, "Spirituality and Liberation," *The Month* (April 1983): 120.

because the painful realities of inward spiritual struggle haunt the pages. Nowadays, Herbert is considered to be one of the greatest English poets. He is also a major figure in the emergence of a distinctive Anglican spirituality during the seventeenth century. Herbert would not have used the word *Anglican* to describe himself or his religious tradition. The word seems to be a nineteenth-century invention.

Herbert is said to have described his poetic collection *The Temple* to his close friend Nicholas Ferrar (founder of the quasi-monastic Little Gidding community) as "a picture of the many spiritual conflicts that have passed betwixt God and my soul before I could subject mine to the will of Jesus my Master: in which service I have now found perfect freedom."[23] Even if the personal tone of these words is authentic, it is widely agreed that *The Temple*, published in 1633 shortly after Herbert's death, also has a conscious structure as a work of religious teaching. While many of the poems are almost certainly genuine expressions of Herbert's own experience, their purpose is not essentially autobiographical in our modern sense. For Herbert, personal experience was simply a rhetorical device by means of which God could be communicated to the reader, who would then be led to greater praise and to a deeper response.

The scheme of the poems in *The Temple* is closely ordered. They are gathered into a three-part structure entitled "The Church Porch," "The Church," and "The Church Militant." Of these three parts, the middle part is by far the largest. This central collection is also spiritually the richest and the most dynamic. The titles of the three sections correspond to the three different meanings of *temple* or *church*. First of all, it is a physical building within which God is somehow present. Some of Herbert's poems employ features of the church building as a framework for teaching. Examples are "The Altar," "The Church Floor," "The Windows," and "Church Monuments." In doing this, the poems underline the importance of order and beauty in the Christian life. The temple is secondly the Body of Christ, that is, the Christian community. Thus, other poems in the collection express the

---

[23] This supposed quote of Herbert's own words is included in the seventeenth-century *The Life of Mr. George Herbert* by Izaak Walton, which is no longer in print.

church's liturgical year or the services through which the community expresses and builds its identity. Examples include "Evensong," "Mattins," "Lent," and "Holy Communion." Finally, the temple is the individual human person, described by St. Paul as the "temple of the Holy Spirit" (1 Cor 3:16).

This final emphasis on the individual person points to an important aspect of George Herbert's teaching. *The Temple* is clearly meant to communicate to readers the Christian spiritual path. However, the poems are not primarily a collection of instructions. There is something morally exhortative about "The Church Porch," the first of the three sections of *The Temple*. However, this is not true of the lyrical poems in the extensive central section, "The Church." Stylistically, most of the poems in this section are addressed to God and therefore take the form of meditation or intimate conversation. The poems seek to move the reader to make a feeling response to God and therefore ultimately to adopt a change of life. Precisely because the poems lay bare George Herbert's own spiritual life for the sake of other people, they also identify with the problems and aspirations experienced by all Christians.

One example of the key elements of a spiritual life, and some striking writing on prayer, occurs in the poem entitled "Prayer I." This extraordinary sonnet has no main verb but consists of a succession of metaphors. Thus, its impact relies on a cumulative effect rather than on a final, conclusive definition. Metaphor provides Herbert with a greater imaginative scope that enables him to move beyond the limits of the expressible. Paradoxically, therefore, George Herbert offers many images of prayer and yet at the same time suggests an underlying truth that prayer, as a way of enshrining our relationship with God, cannot be definitively described. Prayer is a mysterious process that enables us to touch ultimate mystery.

> Prayer the Church's banquet, Angel's age,
>   God's breath in man returning to his birth,
>   The soul in paraphrase, heart in pilgrimage,
> The Christian plummet sounding heav'n and earth;
> Engine against th'Almighty, sinner's tower,
>   Reversed thunder, Christ-side-piercing spear,
>   The six-days world transposing in an hour,

A kind of tune, which all things hear and fear;
Softness and peace, and joy, and love, and bliss,
    Exalted Manna, gladness of the best,
    Heaven in ordinary, man well drest,
The milky way, the bird of Paradise,
    Church-bells beyond the stars heard, the soul's blood,
    The land of spices; something understood.

In prayer, it is possible to be transported, even if only momentarily, to another realm. The words "Angel's age," "the milky way," and a tune "beyond the stars" suggest that prayer touches the infinite. The poem concludes with the words "something understood." This suggests a profound yet elusive encounter with the mysterious otherness of God.[24]

The themes of spiritual desire and of inner struggle, and the connections between them, are beautifully portrayed in Herbert's poems. In *The Temple*, Herbert emphasizes that human beings are creatures of desire who (as Herbert himself appears to do in his poetry) struggle to reach out to God in response to God's own dynamic of love and desire. In his notable prose work on the life and work of a priest, *The Country Parson*, Herbert speaks of God as the one "who giveth me my desires and performances." In the poem "Discipline" (verse 2), Herbert affirms,

For my heart's desire
Unto Thine is bent:
    I aspire
To a full consent.

In terms of God, God's freedom and activity are most powerfully expressed by Herbert not in terms of divine judgment but rather as love. In the poem "Love (1)," God is described as "Immortal Love," and in another poem, "Love (2)," God's love is imaged as "Immortal

---

[24] For a selection of Herbert's writings with commentary, see Philip Sheldrake, ed., *Heaven in Ordinary: George Herbert and His Writings* (London: Canterbury Press, 2009). See also Rowell, Stevenson, and Williams, *Love's Redeeming Work*; William Countryman, *The Poetic Imagination: An Anglican Spiritual Tradition* (London: Darton, Longman & Todd, 1999).

Heat" whose "flame" arouses true desires in us. Herbert's poem "Evensong" (named for the Church of England service that is the equivalent of Vespers) opens with the phrase "Blest be the God of love," and verse 4 concludes:

> My God, thou art all love.
> Not one poor minute scapes thy breast
> But brings a favour from above;
> And in this love, more than in bed, I rest.

God woos us sensitively. Although Herbert struggled with the idea, his fundamental assurance is always God's love rather than God's anger. Indeed God's loving desire is more powerful in its effects than judgmental anger could ever be:

> Then let wrath remove;
> Love will do the deed:
>   For with love
> Stony hearts will bleed. ("Discipline," verse 5)

One of the most striking of Herbert's poems in relation to human intimacy with God is entitled "Clasping of Hands." In it our deep human desire is described in terms of a union between ourselves and God that somehow transcends the notions of "thine" and "mine."

> O be mine still! Still make me Thine!
> Or rather make no Thine and Mine

It appears that Herbert's desire for God, as is typical of all human beings, was not straightforward. According to the words already noted, and apparently quoted from Herbert's letter to his friend Ferrar, that accompanied his poetry prior to its publication, the poems are an outline of the many spiritual conflicts that Herbert experienced in his relationship with God before he was able to surrender "to the will of Jesus my Master: in whose service I have now found perfect freedom." Indeed, a notable thread running through all of Herbert's poems is a relationship with God characterized by an intense inner spiritual struggle on the part of the human heart. The human heart is a place of conflicting desire:

A wonder tortur'd in the space
Betwixt this world and that of grace. ("Affliction," 4)

There are various dimensions to Herbert's spiritual struggle. There is the classical Protestant sense of sinfulness and unworthiness, including an inability to cope with the single-pointedness of God's unconditional desire and love. However, in my view, the spiritual struggle is more complicated. While Herbert's inner struggle is evident throughout the poetic collection, arguably the most powerful and beautiful expression is the final poem of the central section of *The Temple*, entitled "Love (3)." Here, God (named as Love) welcomes the human character at the heart of the poem (no doubt George Herbert himself). Love invites Herbert to join the feast. This is clearly a reference to the eschatological banquet, but it is widely recognized to have strong eucharistic echoes. This is underlined by the fact that the Gloria, which was recited immediately after Communion in the Book of Common Prayer, appears immediately after the poem. Herbert comes across as desperately wanting to be worthy to be present at the feast. His instinctive desire is to merit God's love. In this final poem of the central section of *The Temple*, what is lacking at God's feast is "A guest . . . worthy to be here." Indeed, a basic question throughout the poetic collection is how Herbert is to let go spiritually, to surrender himself and allow God freely to love him and to serve him. Basically, this human desire to be worthy is a subtle form of pride. On the one hand, it seems entirely appropriate to desire to be worthy before God. However, on the other hand, to do so is to place our own capacities at the center of our relationship rather than God's own freely expressed desire. In this powerful poem God is shown to be the one who respects human beings. Nothing is forced or imposed upon us. However, God desires to grant us everything. In the end, Herbert surrenders his own desires, including the desire to be worthy of God, and accepts God's desire for him to enter the banquet and to sit down and eat. In that realization and surrender, Herbert finds spiritual freedom.

Just before World War II, the French Jewish philosopher and political activist Simone Weil, who had an inclination toward Christianity and an interest in the mystical, read "Love (3)" while she was staying at the Abbey of Solesmes over Easter. She subsequently used the poem regularly for meditation, and it apparently led her to a powerful mystical experience of the loving presence of Jesus Christ.

> Love bade me welcome: yet my soul drew back
>   Guilty of dust and sin.
> But quick-ey'd Love, observing me grow slack
>   From my first entrance in,
> Drew nearer to me, sweetly questioning,
>   If I lack'd anything.
>
> A guest, I answer'd, worthy to be here:
>   Love said, you shall be he.
> I the unkind, ungrateful? Ah my dear,
>   I cannot look on thee.
> Love took my hand, and smiling did reply,
>   Who made the eyes but I?
>
> Truth Lord, but I have marr'd them: let my shame
>   Go where it doth deserve.
> And know you not, says Love, who bore the blame?
>   My dear, then I will serve.
> You must sit down says Love, and taste my meat:
>   So I did sit and eat. ("Love 3")

George Herbert was a person with deep aesthetic sensibilities.[25] Apart from the beauty of liturgy and of church buildings, Herbert had a great love of music and was himself an able musician. The last two lines of his poem "Church Music" speak of religious music in these terms:

> But if I travel in your company,
> You know the way to heaven's door.

Overall, musical images abound in *The Temple*. In the poem "Easter," Herbert greets the risen Lord with an image of playing the lute. Herbert also thought of poetry as itself a form of prayer, even if sometimes poetry seems hardly adequate to praise God.

---

[25] On Herbert's approach to beauty, music, and poetry, see Sheldrake, *Heaven in Ordinary*, "Beauty, Music and Poetry," 90–94.

To write a verse or two is all the praise
That I can raise. ("Praise 1")

However, Herbert also declares that poetry is a means of communion
with God.

But it is that which while I use
I am with thee. ("The Quiddity")

Behind George Herbert's aesthetics lies a sense of the beauty of God.
In that sense the beauty of creation and of human creativity reflects
the beauty of God. Humankind's great gift is to discern the presence
of God in all things. Therefore, to praise the beauty of human activities such as music-making or writing poetry is also to praise God,
even if beauty created by humans is merely a pale reflection of God's
beauty.

True beauty dwells on high: ours is a flame
But borrow'd thence to light us thither. ("The Forerunners")

Also, while Herbert loved music deeply, in the end:

Christ is my only head
My alone only heart and breast,
My only music. ("Aaron")

Conclusion

In my estimation, the Way of Beauty, while less familiar in conventional studies of Christian spirituality, is a particularly powerful
type of spirituality, whether expressed in nature, visual art, architectural design, music, or literature—particularly, but not exclusively,
in poetry. This Way of Beauty has had an important role in the history
of Christian spirituality, even though it has been regularly overlooked
or underestimated in conventional studies. Hopefully this chapter
will help to restore the balance and to reestablish beauty of all kinds
as a vital expression of the human spiritual quest.

CHAPTER SIX

The Prophetic Way

In this chapter I now wish to consider a fifth and final type of Christian spirituality, which I call the Prophetic Way. As noted in chapter 1, this type of spirituality goes beyond a spirituality of practical action in the everyday world to focus upon critical social action and social justice as a spiritual task. In the opening chapter I suggested that while historic spiritualities have always had prophetic elements, at least implicitly, an overt focus on social justice as a fundamental spiritual issue rather than a purely political task has its roots in the late nineteenth century and was developed most fully during the last fifty years of the twentieth century.

Background: Spirituality and Social Transformation

First, it is important to summarize how a close relationship between Christian spirituality and social transformation is approached. Importantly, it depends on how the public realm is valued. From its scriptural foundations, Christianity is clear that there is no exclusively private "self." To be human necessarily embodies a social identity. For example, the great late-fourth-century theologian St. Augustine (354–430 CE) was clear that our individual lives are intrinsically related to "the common good." In his *Commentary on Genesis*, Adam's sin was to live for himself alone. In contrast, for St. Augustine, the eternal Heavenly City would be a community based on sharing and solidarity.

The mystical dimension of Christian spirituality, outlined in chapter 3, also has profound social implications.[1] One of the great medieval mystical writers, the fourteenth-century Flemish priest Jan van Ruusbroec, interpreted the contemplative life as "the life common to all." Human beings were joined to each other in the service of everyone. Action and contemplation were part of a single whole. The "spiritually elevated" person is nevertheless a "common" person who "owes himself to all those who seek his help."[2] Such a person "goes out towards all creatures . . . in virtue and in works of righteousness."[3] Ruusbroec was also clear that people who practiced contemplative inwardness but disregarded the demands of charity and ethics were guilty of spiritual wickedness.

However, explicit attention to social transformation as a spiritual issue was, as already noted, a particular characteristic of the late twentieth century. The Spanish theologian Gaspar Martinez suggests that what he calls "worldly theologies," especially political and liberation theologies, are simultaneously the ones that place the greatest emphasis on spirituality.[4]

It is possible to argue that historic religions have always had prophetic elements. For example, the prophets of the Hebrew Bible, such as Amos, Isaiah, and Jeremiah, regularly critiqued corrupt social and political systems. In medieval Christian spirituality, the movement associated with St. Francis of Assisi emphasized spiritual poverty and work with marginalized groups of people, partly in reaction against what Francis saw as the prevailing sins of his own wealthy merchant class. However, neither biblical prophecy nor Francis of Assisi explicitly promoted a spirituality of social justice or social transformation.

[1] See the excellent collection of essays in Janet Ruffing, ed., *Mysticism and Social Transformation* (Syracuse, NY: Syracuse University Press, 2001).

[2] For an English translation of Ruusbroec's mystical writings, see Wiseman, *John Ruusbroec*.

[3] *The Spiritual Espousals*, book I, part 2, chapter lxv, in Wiseman, *John Ruusbroec*.

[4] Gaspar Martinez, *Confronting the Mystery of God: Political, Liberation and Public Theologies* (New York: Continuum, 2001).

Context for the Prophetic Way

The explicit development of the Prophetic Way during the twentieth century was the result of several factors, some of which go back to the late nineteenth century. First, there was the birth of what became known as Catholic social teaching in which, over some eighty years, the Roman Catholic Church, through a range of papal encyclicals, developed an official body of teachings on social, political, and economic issues. In 1891, Pope Leo XIII wrote the first such encyclical, *Rerum Novarum*, subtitled The Conditions of the Working Classes. This took a strong stand against laissez-faire capitalism, which was seen as the cause of the misery of so many people of the working classes. The encyclical critiqued the notion that labor is merely a commodity and that wages should be determined solely by market forces without any sense of a morally reasonable minimum wage. While Pope Leo continued to support private property, he also saw it as the duty of the state to protect the interests of the poor. Forty years later, in 1931, the encyclical *Quadragesimo Anno* by Pope Pius XI was even more robust and specific in its moral outrage at economic exploitation and the deficiencies of liberal capitalism. It introduced the notion of sin as potentially collective and social rather than purely individual and personal. Consequently, moral reform should also be social-structural. These two foundational encyclicals were reinforced by a 1949 address by Pope Pius XII, the writings of Pope John XXIII and Pope Paul VI (including his 1967 encyclical *Populorum Progressio*), the Second Vatican Council, especially the Pastoral Constitution on the Church in the Modern World (*Gaudium et Spes*), the document "Justice in the World" of the 1971 Roman Synod, the encyclicals *Laborem Exercens* (1981) and *Centissimus Annus* (1991) of Pope John Paul II, the encyclical *Caritas in Veritate* (2009) of Pope Benedict XVI, and most recently by the strongly worded encyclical by Pope Francis, *Laudato Si'*, with its biting critique of consumerism and environmental degradation.[5] It is worth noting that there is also a substantial tradi-

---

[5] For the texts of major Catholic social encyclicals with commentaries and a substantial introduction, see Kenneth Himes, *Modern Catholic Social Teaching: Commentaries and Interpretations* (Washington, DC: Georgetown University Press, 2005).

tion of Anglican social thought going back to the nineteenth century that in many ways echoes Roman Catholic approaches.[6]

The twentieth century also experienced a range of politically and humanly challenging events that demanded the development of a robust prophetic spirituality. I am talking about the appalling slaughter of two world wars, oppressive totalitarianism (Nazism, Fascism, and Stalinism), the unspeakable Holocaust, and then the birth of the atomic-nuclear age. Together these events provoked an overwhelming sense of the destructive power of war and human oppression. In addition, there was also the gradual and often violent end to European colonialism in Africa, Asia, and Latin America. Finally, there was a growing wave of social-cultural change in Europe and North America in relation to the status and role of women, civil rights for ethnic minorities, and attitudes toward other marginalized groups. In Christianity there have been a range of examples of prophetic spirituality. These include Dietrich Bonhoeffer's radical Christian resistance to the Nazis, the preaching of Martin Luther King Jr. at the heart of the American civil rights movement, feminist spirituality, political theology, and the birth of what is known as "liberation spirituality" in central and Latin America in the 1970s. This eventually took other forms in Africa and Asia.

Overall, the twentieth century was a period of immense social, cultural, and religious change. Commentators speak of a transition from "modernity" to "postmodernity." Modernity is associated with a worldview, originating in the Enlightenment and consolidated by the technological advances of the Industrial Revolution, that promoted the power of human reason to address any question. With this went an ordered view of the world and a confident belief in inexorable human progress. At the beginning of the twentieth century, this sense of a rational, stable world seemed impregnable. Yet the seeds of radical change were already present. For example, evolutionary theory suggested that human existence could no longer be separated from the remainder of nature's processes. The writings of Karl Marx challenged fixed notions of society. The birth of psychology suggested

---

[6] See, for example, the recent collection of essays by Anglican and Roman Catholic writers, Malcolm Brown, ed., *Anglican Social Theology: Renewing the Vision Today* (London: Church House, 2014).

that human motivation is complex and called into question the objectivity of human reason.

The twentieth century also saw the development of rapid international travel and a communications revolution (radio, television, and then information technology). Thanks to global communications and new technologies, events had worldwide immediacy and impact, information exchange became virtually instantaneous, and change consequently happened with a previously unimaginable rapidity.

Thus, postmodernity defines a new world where the simple, optimistic answers of a previous age are no longer possible. By the close of the twentieth century, fixed systems of thought and behavior had fragmented and the world was understood as radically plural. In an increasingly globalized world, religious and ethnic diversity is now identified as the fundamental reality of human existence.

The major social, political, and cultural changes had a serious impact on Christian spirituality. Three elements stand out. First, in the Western world, institutional religion has noticeably declined alongside a wider loss of faith in traditional authoritative institutions. Second, the hard boundaries within Christianity and between Christianity and other world religions began to erode. The ecumenical movement emerged in the early twentieth century and by the end of the century had extended into wider interreligious dialogue. Third, Christianity became truly global. Europe and North America were no longer the sole arbiters of what counts as Christian spirituality.

It is too early to make a definitive assessment of the future of Christian spirituality. We cannot predict which themes and values will endure, which individuals will be seen as spiritual giants in a hundred years' time, which movements will have become enduring traditions, which writings will have become classics. At this point, it is possible to select only a few people and movements that capture the new spirit of Christian spirituality. Therefore, to illustrate the Prophetic Way, I will first focus briefly on several significant spiritual figures and movements. Finally, I will take liberation theology and spirituality, and particularly Gustavo Gutiérrez, as the main paradigm.

Charles de Foucauld (1858–1916)

My first spiritual figure is Charles de Foucauld. It was in the period after 1901 that he made his lasting impact on Christian spirituality.

Born into a French aristocratic family, de Foucauld's early adult life was somewhat hedonistic. He abandoned religious faith, spent money wildly, lived a dandified life, became a soldier, was posted to Algeria, and then resigned his commission when asked to give up his mistress. This relationship soon ended, and de Foucauld went to Morocco in disguise and explored what was then a closed country. On his return to France in 1886, de Foucauld was awarded a gold medal by the French Geographical Society for his Morocco report. He also underwent a religious reconversion under the influence of the famous spiritual guide Abbé Henri Huvelin.

De Foucauld had developed strong feelings about desert solitude, and to this was now added a strong devotion to the person of Jesus and to the Eucharist. Initially, he became a Cistercian monk in France and then Syria, but after a few years he sought something spiritually more demanding. From 1897 he lived as a hermit and gardener attached to a Poor Clare convent in Nazareth. After being ordained in France in 1901, de Foucauld moved back to the Sahara Desert, where he settled first at Beni Abbes and then at Tamanrasset in southern Algeria. There he lived among the Tuareg people, not seeking to convert them but studying their culture and seeking to serve their needs. He lived a solitary contemplative life based on eucharistic devotion and meditative scriptural prayer. De Foucauld conceived the idea of founding a new religious community, but this did not happen during his lifetime. Tragically, he was killed by Bedouin tribesmen in 1916 during an uprising against the French colonial power. Charles de Foucauld was beatified by Pope Benedict XVI in 2005.

After his death, Frère Charles de Jésus, as he was known, became the inspiration for a new spiritual movement and eventually for the foundation of several religious communities, notably the Little Brothers and Sisters of Jesus. After World War II, these small semimonastic groups developed a distinctive profile. They lived in apartments in small groups in the poorest parts of Western cities as well as in areas of the developing world. Like Charles de Foucauld, the Little Brothers and Sisters do not undertake explicit social action. However, they live in radical solidarity among their neighbors by being a hospitable presence while supporting themselves by working in ordinary jobs mixed with periods of common prayer and silence.[7]

---

[7] See Ellsberg, *Charles de Foucauld.*

Dietrich Bonhoeffer (1906–1945)

Another notable example of prophetic spirituality is Dietrich Bon-hoeffer. A German Protestant pastor and theologian from a prominent intellectual and artistic family in Breslau, he was executed by the Nazis. Bonhoeffer was sharply critical of the church's lack of political engagement during the Nazi era. He has become an iconic figure of resistance to dictatorship and of political martyrdom. Probably his best-known work of spirituality is *The Cost of Discipleship*, in which he outlines the painful consequences of following a Christian spiritual path.[8] For Bonhoeffer, costly discipleship implied both a disciplined life of prayer and critical engagement with surrounding social and political realities. Although a pacifist, Bonhoeffer became involved in anti-Nazi activities. In prophetic contrast to the surrender of the institutional church, Bonhoeffer was the inspiration behind an alter-native community of those who resisted Nazi control of the state church. After he returned from a visit to England in 1935, Bonhoeffer led an unofficial seminary at Finkenwalde, where he also formed a quasi-monastic community inspired by his experiences of Anglican communities such as Mirfield.

From around 1932, Bonhoeffer had begun to practice daily scrip-tural meditation. It is interesting that he called his first attempts *Exerzitien*, which for Protestants of that time had clear echoes of Ignatius Loyola. While controversial, Bonhoeffer appears to have believed that an important spiritual tool had been lost by Protestants and needed to be revived. Bonhoeffer's library from this period sur-vives and includes a copy of the Ignatian *Spiritual Exercises*. Some of this experience found its way into his book *Life Together*, written for the Finkenwalde community, in its teaching on disciplined and regular Bible reading and meditation as the basis for community life.

While Bonhoeffer had the opportunity to settle in the United States, where he went to teach in 1939, he voluntarily returned to Germany before the war started in order, as he said to friends, to share in the trials of German Christians. Arrested by the Gestapo in 1943, Bonhoeffer spent the last two years of his life in prison, from where he wrote many letters—including letters of spiritual guidance for his students. These were eventually edited and published and have be-

---

[8] See Dietrich Bonhoeffer, *The Cost of Discipleship* (New York: Touchstone, 1995).

come a spiritual classic known as *Letters and Papers from Prison.*[9] In them, Bonhoeffer's plea for a "religionless Christianity" was a further prophetic stage in his opposition to the way in which public religion had, in his estimation, replaced the demands of a costly commitment to a living God.

In someone like Bonhoeffer, the mystic becomes the political martyr. The eminent German theologian Jürgen Moltmann comments in reference to Bonhoeffer, "The place of mystical experience is in very truth the cell—the prison cell. The 'witness to the truth of Christ' is despised, scoffed at, persecuted, dishonoured and rejected. In his own fate he experiences the fate of Christ. His fate conforms to Christ's fate. That is what the mystics called *conformitas crucis*, the conformity of the cross. . . . Eckhart's remark that suffering is the shortest way to the birth of God in the soul applies, not to any imagined suffering, but to the very real sufferings endured by 'the witness to the truth.' "[10] Bonhoeffer was executed in 1945, just before the war's end, at Flossenbürg concentration camp.[11]

Dorothy Day (1897–1980)

Dorothy Day offers a third example of the Prophetic Way. She was one of the most influential figures in the English-speaking world in promoting a spirituality of social justice. Born in Brooklyn, New York, to nonreligious parents, Day initially committed herself after university to radical thought and mixed in both Communist and anarchist-syndicalist circles. She became a labor activist and a journalist and was arrested several times. Day lived in New York with her partner, with whom she had a child. It was during her pregnancy that she converted to Roman Catholicism. This, and the baptism of her child, led to the breakup of her relationship. Day became convinced that Christianity answered the shortcomings she had increasingly experienced in revolutionary circles. While radical politics had identified the causes of alienation in modern society, the teachings of Christianity

[9] See Dietrich Bonhoeffer, *Letters and Papers from Prison* (New York: Touchstone, 1997).

[10] Moltmann, *Experiences of God*, 72.

[11] See Geffrey B. Kelly and F. Burton Nelson, *The Cost of Moral Leadership: The Spirituality of Dietrich Bonhoeffer* (Grand Rapids, MI: Eerdmans, 2003).

concerning disinterested love and inclusive community pointed toward a solution. Day soon met a French expatriate philosopher, Peter (Pierre) Maurin, who became her spiritual mentor. Maurin guided her reading and offered her a vision of pacifism and close identification with the poor. In 1933, during the Great Depression, they together began the Catholic Worker Movement.

The Catholic Worker, a newspaper that documented workers' struggles and proclaimed a social gospel, promoted a spirituality of prophetic social witness and pacifism. Catholic Worker spirituality, as conceived by Day and Maurin, offered an alternative to secular Marxism in its communitarian and personalist philosophy. Based on the Gospel of Matthew, chapter 25, Christ was to be experienced as present in all those in need. Every human being, without exception, had a unique and equal dignity. The heart of Christian living was radical community. This was not a community detached from surrounding reality. Rather, it was called upon to undertake prophetic action on behalf of the oppressed. Indeed, for Day, there could be no authentic Christian spirituality that did not have social justice at its core.

The active spirituality of the Catholic Worker Movement led to the foundation of houses of hospitality that offer a haven for all kinds of marginalized people. These currently number over two hundred across the United States. Most are in poor urban neighborhoods, although some are rural. The movement has an entirely lay membership whose rule of life centers on common prayer and the Eucharist. Day was particularly inspired by the regular reading of Scripture, the Rule of St. Benedict, the teachings of Francis of Assisi on voluntary poverty, and the "little way" of Thérèse of Lisieux. While not radically revolutionary, the movement was discomforting for many in the church and attracted opposition. Members not only served the poor but also undertook direct action against injustice where needed. Day herself continued through World War II, the Cold War, and the Vietnam War to advocate pacifism and to undertake acts of civil disobedience. While she was highly controversial for much of her life, by the time of her death in 1980 Day was widely admired, and more recently her canonization has been proposed.[12]

---

[12] See Ellsberg, *Dorothy Day*.

Thomas Merton (1915–1968)

As a contemplative monk, Thomas Merton may seem a less obvious example of the Prophetic Way. Merton has been described as one of the greatest spiritual writers of the twentieth century. Born in France of mixed New Zealand and American parentage, Merton had an insecure and unhappy childhood. His mother died when he was six, and his artist father neglected him and died when Merton was fifteen. He was educated at an English boarding school, at Cambridge University, and then at Columbia University in New York and, perhaps not surprisingly, led a somewhat self-centered life. He fathered a child at Cambridge, but both mother and child are said to have died in the London Blitz during World War II. Consequently, the motivation for his intense religious conversion in 1941 to Roman Catholicism and entry into the reformed Cistercians (Trappists) is complex. He remained a monk of Gethsemani Abbey in Kentucky (as Father Louis) until his premature death in 1968 in an accident during a visit to Thailand in pursuit of Christian-Buddhist dialogue.

Merton is variously remembered for his attempts to rearticulate contemplative-monastic life and the Christian mystical tradition for a contemporary audience, for his literary talent as essayist, poet, and diarist, for his ecumenical friendships, for his special contribution to Christian-Buddhist dialogue, and for his later commitment to issues of social justice and world peace. Merton was a searcher and a wanderer who, in his monastic cell, journeyed onward from the initially narrow church-centered spirituality of his autobiography, *The Seven Storey Mountain* (1948), to radical reflections on the public world in *Conjectures of a Guilty Bystander* (1966).

Merton's writing was regularly autobiographical, even when the focus was not on himself but on contemplation, monastic life, interreligious dialogue, or social justice. This made Merton's readers companions on his journey. Merton remained committed to his original option for a countercultural lifestyle but reinterpreted this through a growing conviction that, in the face of an individualistic culture, the true self exists only in solidarity with the other. The authentic self is vulnerable rather than protected behind walls of separation and spiritual superiority. This growing insight led to a second conversion experience in Louisville, the town near his monastery, in the early

1960s. Merton was overwhelmed by a sense of unity with all the people on the sidewalks. This provoked in him a different sense of relationship to the world: "It was like waking from a dream of separateness, of spurious self-isolation in a special world, the world of renunciation and supposed holiness. The whole illusion of a separate holy existence is a dream. . . . This sense of liberation from an illusory difference [between monastic life and ordinary people] was such a relief and such a joy to me that I almost laughed aloud."[13] This reconversion produced a strong sense (expressed in *Life and Holiness* in 1964) that the spiritual life is a question not of withdrawal but of an awareness of a common responsibility for the future of humanity. Three things came together for Merton. First, he was increasingly attracted to a life of radical solitude within the monastic property. Second, without losing his concern for the contemplative-mystical tradition, he increasingly embraced a prophetic stance in his prolific writings, even though it risked unpopularity with some of his American readership; Merton supported the civil rights movement, criticized the Cold War, opposed nuclear weapons, and joined the anti–Vietnam War lobby. Third, Merton's long-standing interest in Buddhism blossomed into active involvement in interreligious dialogue, particularly with the Japanese Zen Buddhist Suzuki and, toward the end of his life, with the Dalai Lama.[14]

Political Spiritualities

Turning now from individuals to prophetic movements, the political, feminist, and liberationist expressions of spirituality promote two central and interdependent values. First, authentic spirituality necessarily demands that humanity should engage fearlessly with structures of injustice and violence. This includes the concept of structural sin—that is, evil and sin are never purely personal but are frequently expressed in the structures of society.[15] Second, a truly

---

[13] Merton, *Conjectures of a Guilty Bystander*, 140–41.

[14] See Cunningham, *Thomas Merton: Spiritual Master* and *Thomas Merton and the Monastic Vision*.

[15] See José Ignacio González Faus, chapter 1, "Sin," in Jon Sobrino and Ignacio Ellacuría, eds., *Systematic Theology: Perspectives from Liberation Theology* (Maryknoll, NY: Orbis Books, 1996), 194–204.

effective commitment to promoting social justice cannot be purely political. It demands the purification of our human motivation through the challenging practice of contemplation.

Late twentieth-century European political theology focuses on how to engage explicitly with political and social structures. Its key exponents, such as the Roman Catholic Johannes Baptist Metz and the Protestants Dorothee Sölle and Jürgen Moltmann, also engage in striking ways with mysticism and spirituality.[16] Sölle was deeply inspired by the Christian mystical tradition. For her, resistance and changing the world must be rooted in the spiritual. Mystical consciousness "tears the veil of triviality" because it is touched by the spirit of life. "Without reinspiration, nothing new begins." There is then a leaving of a focus on the self that leads to "a living in God."[17] The *via unitiva*, or mystical path, involves healing as the birth of true social resistance. For Sölle, we become capable of healing others only insofar as we, too, are healed.

From a different theological perspective, Jürgen Moltmann, in his short book *Experiences of God*, writes about the ethical dimension of mystical wisdom. However, the most interesting aspect of his approach to contemplation is the description of a fivefold contemplative process to replace the more traditional threefold way. This process is a continuous circular movement. It begins with our engagement with the ambiguities of the world. Our instinct is to want to change things. However, action for change inevitably leads to a realization that a truly Christian response must be embedded in contemplation. Contemplation, focused on Jesus Christ in the gospels, leads to a movement away from self and from false images of God toward the classic Reformation, "God alone." Our encounter with the living God, purified of selfishness, is what Western mysticism classically describes as "union." However, this is not an end in itself. The purpose of mystical union is not merely spiritual experience. What is encountered at the heart of God is the cross. Consequently, union leads to a deeper identification with the person of Jesus, who poured himself out in kenotic love. So, the mystical journey makes union a new point

---

[16] For an overview, see Martinez, *Confronting the Mystery of God*.

[17] Dorothee Sölle, "To be Amazed, to Let Go, to Resist: Outline for a Mystical Journey Today," in Ruffing, *Mysticism and Social Transformation*, 45–51.

of departure leading to a renewed practice of everyday discipleship and social engagement. Moltmann wrote, "As long as we do not think that dying with Christ spiritually is a substitute for dying with him in reality, mysticism does not mean estrangement from action; it is a preparation for public, political discipleship."[18] The mystical-contemplative icon therefore becomes the political martyr, such as Bonhoeffer, as much as the monk.

Feminist Spiritualities

Another important prophetic spirituality is feminist spirituality. The word *feminism* appears to have been used first in the 1880s and from the start had close religious connections (for example, in challenges to male interpretations of Scripture in *The Woman's Bible*, which appeared 1895–1898). The first wave of feminism resulted in women in Western Europe and North America gaining the right to vote, own property, and be awarded university degrees. A further stage of feminism arose from the political upheavals in Europe in the late 1960s and from the civil rights movement in the United States, in both of which women played a prominent part. By the 1970s and 1980s, feminist studies appeared as an academic discipline, offering a critical analysis of gender stereotyping and its impact on women's identities and roles. This soon began to influence Christian theology and spirituality in ways that continue today. Notable examples of theologians who have had a particular role in developing a feminist approach to Christian spirituality are Sandra Schneiders, Joann Wolski Conn, Rosemary Radford Ruether, Elizabeth Johnson, Catherine LaCugna, Anne Carr, and Dorothee Sölle (all in North America), Elisabeth Moltmann-Wendell in Germany, and Mary Grey and Grace Jantzen in the United Kingdom.

A fundamental insight of feminist spirituality is that everyone's relationship with God and approaches to spiritual practice are deeply influenced by how gender is constructed within a given culture. The first step in feminist spiritualities is to identify fundamental ways in which people's humanity is undermined. Feminist spirituality sug-

---

[18] Jürgen Moltmann, "The Theology of Mystical Experience," *Experiences of God*, 73.

gests that women's identity has been restricted by some elements of traditional spirituality (for example, suspicion of the body, excessive intellectualism, the bypassing of sexuality, and an emphasis on passivity). These limitations are then legitimized by imaging God purely as male. The next step in feminist spirituality, as with all liberation spiritualities, is to reconstruct alternative ways of talking about God and of understanding our relationship with God. The specific nature of women's spiritual experience and ways of relating to God become a vital source of spiritual wisdom. This leads naturally to a deeper reflection on experience in the light of the Scriptures and Christian tradition in place of categories that were often based on unexamined male-clerical assumptions.

The work of feminist Scripture scholars such as Sandra Schneiders, who is sensitive to spirituality, has been an important tool.[19] Equally, the writings of such theologians as Elizabeth Johnson and Catherine LaCugna have offered spiritually rich interpretations of Christian theologies of God with the aim of outlining a more adequate spirituality.[20] In terms of rereading classic Christian spiritual or mystical texts from a feminist perspective, the works of Sölle and of Grace Jantzen are particularly important. Jantzen wrote a major feminist academic study of Christian mysticism, *Power, Gender and Christian Mysticism*.[21] In recent years in the United States of America, new forms of feminist spirituality have appeared applicable specifically to African American experience (known as womanist spirituality) and Hispanic experience (known as *mujerista* spirituality).

Spiritualities of Liberation

Probably the best-known example of the Prophetic Way in modern times is liberation theology and its associated spirituality. This originated in Latin America in the late 1960s and, as we shall see, later

---

[19] See Sandra Schneiders, *The Revelatory Text: Interpreting the New Testament as Sacred Scripture* (Collegeville MN: Liturgical Press, 1999).

[20] See Elizabeth Johnson, *She Who Is: The Mystery of God in Feminist Theological Discourse* (New York: Crossroad, 1996), and Catherine M. LaCugna, *God for Us: The Trinity and Christian Life* (San Francisco: HarperCollins, 1993).

[21] Grace Jantzen, *Power, Gender and Christian Mysticism* (Cambridge: Cambridge University Press, 1995).

took on distinctive forms in Africa and Asia. Liberation theology embraces a range of reflections based on a critique of unjust social structures and the struggle to overcome them. It suggests that the promotion of social justice is integral to any authentic spiritual path. This type of spirituality also questions the ways in which society creates structures that undermine the human dignity of certain categories of people, such as the socially marginalized, the materially poor, or certain ethnic groups. Despite criticisms by some people, the basis for liberation theology and spirituality is not Marxism but rather the Hebrew and Christian Scriptures. Especially important are the book of Exodus, with its theme of God leading the chosen people from exile to the Promised Land, and the theme of redemption in the New Testament gospels.

How we approach the relationship between the Christian life and social engagement obviously depends on our theological evaluation of the outer, social, "public" world. Unfortunately, our Western culture is deeply polarized. The private sphere (inwardness, family and close friends, an idealization of home and domesticity) tends to be privileged as the backstage where the individual is truly him- or herself, relaxing unobserved before putting on various personae that the self needs in order to play out different roles on the stage of public life. However, living in public is not really a matter of a role that it is possible to set aside. If there were a preexistent self, prior to all roles, then social life would be fundamentally detached from our identity. However, the Christian theological tradition underlines the fact that there is no wholly private self. The core of the Christian life is to be united with God in Jesus Christ through a Spirit-led communion with one another. God's own relational nature is fundamental to this life. God-as-Trinity is understood to be "persons in communion," a mutuality of self-giving love. Communion underpins all existence, including human life. The mission of God, the *missio Dei*, is the divine activity of self-disclosure in creation, salvation history, and incarnation drawing all things into the limitless embrace of God's unifying love. The life of discipleship is to participate ever more deeply in God's mission through a faithful following of the way of Jesus, the bearer and expression of God's incoming kingdom.

A number of theological writers in liberationist spirituality have argued that the mystical-contemplative way is a necessary dimension of social engagement. Interestingly, Spanish theologian Gaspar Martinez has suggested that what he calls "worldly theologies," those modern Catholic theologies engaged explicitly with the public dimensions of life, are simultaneously the ones that focus most sharply on the mystery of God, with a greater rather than a lesser emphasis on spirituality and mysticism. He notes in particular Johannes Baptist Metz, Gustavo Gutiérrez, and David Tracy—significantly, all of them inspired in different ways by Karl Rahner (although we should also note the writings of Edward Schillebeeckx in this regard).

A key concept in liberationist spirituality is that God's love, while all-embracing and nonexclusive, is manifested in different ways. God's love is inherently disturbing and always challenges people to change. The "poor" are to be empowered rather than to allow themselves to be passive victims or passive recipients of the goodwill of those more fortunate than themselves. The "rich" (whether materially wealthy or socially dominant) are called upon to recognize their need for conversion in order to embrace solidarity with everyone.

In classic Latin American liberation theology, there have been many points of connection with a spirituality of social justice, for example in the writings of Jon Sobrino, Leonardo Boff, and Pedro Casaldáliga, and in the comprehensive multiauthor volume *Mysterium Liberationis: Fundamental Concepts of Liberation Theology*.[22] In terms of the intersection of liberation theology and feminist spirituality, the Cuban American theologian Ada María Isasi-Díaz is a notable example, not least as an expression of *mujerista* spirituality in the United States. This approach affirms that true spirituality is not disembodied interiority but should be marked by a struggle against the sexism, ethnic prejudice, and economic oppression that diminishes the life experience of Latina women.[23] The Peruvian theologian Gustavo Gutiérrez has become another iconic figure within the liberationist

---

[22] For example, Jon Sobrino, *Spirituality of Liberation: Towards Political Holiness* (Maryknoll, NY: Orbis Books, 1988); Leonardo Boff, *Saint Francis: A Model of Human Liberation* (London: SCM Press, 1982); Pedro Casaldáliga and José-María Vigil, *Political Holiness: A Spirituality of Liberation* (Maryknoll, NY: Orbis Books, 1994); Ignacio Ellacuría and Jon Sobrino, eds., *Mysterium Liberationis: Fundamental Concepts of Liberation Theology* (Maryknoll, NY: Orbis Books, 1993).

[23] Ada María Isasi-Díaz, *Mujerista Theology: A Theology for the 21st Century* (Maryknoll, NY: Orbis Books, 1996).

tradition, and at the end of this chapter I will briefly explore him as a paradigm of the Prophetic Way.

Chilean theologian Segundo Galilea has written significantly concerning the mystical or contemplative dimensions of political and social responses to injustice. Galilea suggests that there needs to be a movement away from the notion that an effective response is purely ethical or structural. Such a limited approach, Galilea suggests, may all too easily become a new form of oppression. There needs to be a truly spiritual experience of discovering the compassion of God incarnate in the poor. Humans are not able to find true compassion, nor create structures of deep transformation, without first entering contemplatively into Jesus' own compassion. Only contemplative-mystical practice as the foundation of social action is capable of bringing about the change of heart necessary for lasting solidarity and social transformation—particularly a solidarity that is capable of embracing the oppressor as well as the oppressed. Consequently, according to Galilea, social engagement must be accompanied by a process of interior transformation and liberation from self-seeking. This is the heart of what he refers to as "integral liberation."[24]

Galilea calls for a reformulation of the notions of contemplation and the mystical. He suggests that at the heart of the Christian tradition there has always been an understanding of contemplation as a supreme act of self-forgetfulness rather than merely a practice of personal interiority. In the teachings of the great Christian mystics, contemplation is related to the critical Christian theological theme of the cross.

> This implies the crucifixion of egoism and the purification of the self as a condition of contemplation. This crucifixion of egoism in forgetfulness of self in the dialectic prayer-commitment will be brought to fulfilment both in the mystical dimension of communication with Jesus in the luminous night of faith, and also in the sacrifice which is assumed by commitment to the liberation of others. The "death" of mysticism and the "death" of the militant are the two dimensions of the call to accept the cross, as the condition of being a disciple. . . . The desert as a political experience

---

[24] Segundo Galilea, "The Spirituality of Liberation," *The Way* (July 1985): 186–94.

liberates [the Christian] from egoism and from the "system," and
is a source of freedom and of an ability to liberate.[25]

Using different language, Brazilian theologian Leonardo Boff has
sharply criticized the traditional spiritual and monastic formula of
ora et labora (prayer and work) on the grounds that it espouses a kind
of parallelism. At best the *et* has stood for an alternation of interior
prayer and external engagement. Classically, contemplation was
thought to be the source of all value. Social engagement was not a
direct mediation of God and was of value only to the extent that it
was "fed" by contemplation and thus "redeemed" from its secular,
profane associations. [26] Boff notes that in some contemporary Christian approaches to engagement, over-dominated by social and political theory, a parallelism continues to exist but is reversed. Thus,
social engagement predominates over contemplation so that contemplation becomes another, subsidiary, form of social practice. Boff
argues for an equal, dialectical relationship "treating them as two
spaces that are open to one another and imply each other."[27] This
dialectic produces a unity in what Boff calls the "mysticism-politics
relationship." Boff coins a new phrase to describe being contemplative while engaged fully in the public spaces of political transformation: *contemplativus in liberatione*. This unity of prayer-liberation is
based on a living faith in God. Thus the contemplative or the mystical
"is not carried out only in the sacred space of prayer, nor in the sacred
precinct of the church; purified, sustained and nurtured by living
faith, it also finds its place in political and social practice."[28]

As noted earlier, in Africa and Asia, liberation theology and its
associated spirituality has taken distinctive cultural forms while
sharing the fundamental values of its Latin American inspiration. In
Africa there are a range of emphases. For example, Laurenti Magesa
from Tanzania focuses strongly on the injustice of a continent that is
not economically self-sufficient but is the victim of global inequality.

[25] Segundo Galilea, "Liberation as an Encounter with Politics and Contemplation,"
in *Understanding Mysticism*, ed. Richard Woods (London: Athlone, 1980), 535–36.
[26] Leonardo Boff, "The Need for Political Saints: From a Spirituality of Liberation
to the Practice of Liberation," *Cross Currents* 30, no. 4 (Winter 1980–81): 371.
[27] Ibid., 373.
[28] Ibid., 374.

Theology and spirituality need to respond to this situation of dependency not by imitating Western materialism but by building creatively upon the basic African "spirituality of being."[29] However, Magesa is not naïve about traditional African culture. He robustly critiques women's oppression within traditional religious-cultural systems. This issue is also confronted powerfully in the movement of African women's feminist-liberationist theology. For example, the writings of Mercy Amba Oduyoye in Ghana focus critically on how traditional African culture impacts on the religious-spiritual experiences of women.[30] In South Africa, divided by apartheid over many decades, there have been a variety of liberationist theological-spirituality responses. Buti Tlhagale (later the Roman Catholic archbishop of Johannesburg) worked in Soweto and developed a black theology of labor. This seeks to awaken assertiveness in black workers so that they become "self-realised" persons rather than depersonalized objects in the labor market.[31] The Reformed pastor and former African National Congress activist Allan Boesak became known as a liberation theologian during the apartheid era.[32] He is now a vocal critic of all forms of discrimination (including racial discrimination by the governing ANC and anti-gay attitudes in his church) because this undermines the vision of a single nation. He also focuses on a theology of reconciliation, as do Charles Villa-Vicencio, in his call for a reconstructive theology of nation-building, and John de Gruchy, in his work on reconciliation, solidarity, and social justice.[33]

Because of its coexistence with other major world religions, such as Hinduism and Buddhism, Christian spirituality in Asia is often closely associated in people's minds with interreligious dialogue and

[29] See Laurenti Magesa, "Globalisation: African Spirituality," *New People* 80 (Autumn 2002).

[30] See, for example, Mercy Amba Oduyoye, *Beads and Strands: Reflections of an African Woman on Christianity in Africa* (Maryknoll, NY: Orbis Books, 2004).

[31] See Buti Tlhagale, "Towards a Black Theology of Labour," in *Resistance and Hope: South African Essays in Honour of Beyers Naude*, ed. Charles Villa-Vicencio and John W. de Gruchy (Grand Rapids, MI: Eerdmans, 1985).

[32] See Allan Boesak, *Farewell to Innocence: A Socio-Ethical Study on Black Theology and Power* (Maryknoll, NY: Orbis Books, 1978).

[33] See Charles Villa-Vicencio, *A Theology of Reconstruction: Nation-Building and Human Rights* (Cambridge: Cambridge University Press, 1992); see also John W. de Gruchy, *Reconciliation: Restoring Justice* (London: SCM Press, 2002).

even with what became known as "dual belonging" or "double belonging." This is expressed in such statements as "I am a Christian *and* a Hindu" and is represented by such thinkers as the late Raimundo Pannikar, a Roman Catholic priest and philosopher, who was the son of a Hindu father and a Roman Catholic mother. Other prominent examples of interreligious spirituality are the work and writings of Swami Abhishiktananda and Bede Griffiths in India, the Jesuit Aloysius Pieris in Sri Lanka, and the Jesuits Hugo Enomiya-Lassalle, Kakichi Kadowaki, and William Johnston in Japan.[34] However, Asia has also produced its own forms of liberation theology with an associated spirituality.[35] For example, in Sri Lanka Pieris has asserted deep connections between interreligious dialogue and an Asian liberation theology. Another Sri Lankan Roman Catholic theologian and human rights activist, Tissa Balasuriya, portrayed the Virgin Mary, a traditional focus of Catholic devotion, as an image of revolutionary strength rather than docility.[36] A Chinese theologian, Kwok Pui-Lan, recently a professor of theology and spirituality in the United States, has written significantly on the interface of postcolonial and feminist theologies.[37] In India, dalit theology refers to the so-called untouchable castes, who are socially marginalized and traditionally considered by higher castes to be unclean. Dalit spirituality focuses on the restoration of social dignity, an affirmation of the essential equality of all human beings before God, and a strong emphasis on Jesus' proclamation of good news to the poor, freedom for captives, and release for the oppressed (Luke 4). An important image is the suffering of Jesus on the cross and his resurrection as the sources of liberation.[38] My final example of Asian liberation theology and spirituality

[34] On spirituality and interreligious dialogue, see Philip Sheldrake, *Spirituality: A Very Short Introduction* (Oxford: Oxford University Press, 2012), chapter 6, "Spirituality and Religion."

[35] See, for example, Bastiaan Wielanga, "Liberation Theology in Asia," in *The Cambridge Companion to Liberation Theology*, ed. Christopher Rowland (Cambridge: Cambridge University Press, 2007), 55–78.

[36] Tissa Balasuriya, *Mary and Human Liberation: The Story and the Text* (Harrisburg, PA: Trinity, 1997).

[37] For example, Kwok Pui-Lan, *Postcolonial Imagination and Feminist Theology* (London: SCM Press, 2005).

[38] For example, see Peniel Rajkumar, *Dalit Theology and Dalit Liberation* (Farnham, UK: Ashgate, 2010).

is minjung theology in South Korea. This emerged in the 1970s during a period of dictatorship and reflects the struggle for social justice. This "people's theology" seeks to speak both to and on behalf of the oppressed who are ostracized by ruling elites.[39]

The theologies and spiritualities of liberation that have emerged around the world embrace a wide spectrum of reflection and practice based on a critique of all forms of structural injustice and the struggle to overcome it. The characteristic of these spiritualities is that they promote social justice as integral to Christian practice. This approach radically questions the ways in which spirituality has been traditionally presented. Liberation theory, in whatever form, also questions the ways in which both society and the church have created structures that undermine the full human dignity of certain categories of people. Spiritualities of liberation now exist on every continent and focus on issues of economic poverty, racial exclusions, gender inequality, and, more recently, issues of planetary environmental responsibility.

Gustavo Gutiérrez (1928–)

I now want to conclude by briefly exploring the work of Gustavo Gutiérrez as both a leading exponent of Latin American liberation theology and a paradigm of the Prophetic Way of spirituality. Gutiérrez was born into a poor family in Lima, Peru, and suffered severe ill health as a child. Eventually he went to university and then trained as a priest, studying theology in Europe as well as Peru. Ordained in 1959, Gutiérrez worked part-time in the Catholic University and part-time in a poor Lima parish. This dual experience led him to bring together theological reflection and his experience of living with the poor. Gutiérrez played a leading role at the famous conference of Latin American bishops at Medellín in 1967. This translated the thought of Vatican II into the Latin American situation, especially in terms of the promotion of social justice. By 1971 Gutiérrez had published his groundbreaking *A Theology of Liberation*, which set the tone not only for his later works but also for the thinking and writing of a range of other Roman Catholic and Protestant theologians

[39] For example, see Yung Suk Kim and Jin-Ho Kim, eds., *Reading Minjung Theology in the Twenty-First Century* (Eugene, OR: Wipf and Stock, 2013).

on the continent. In 1999 Gutiérrez entered the Dominican Order and remains active as a distinguished professor of theology at the University of Notre Dame.

Gutiérrez specifically developed his approach to spirituality in *We Drink from Our Own Wells*. His spirituality is deeply scriptural. Especially important is the book of Exodus, with its theme of God leading his people out of slavery to the Promised Land—plus the theme of redemption from the New Testament. The book establishes clearly that spirituality, theology, and social practice form a continuum. At the heart of it all is the experience of God speaking in and through the situation of the poor. Theology reflects on this experience in the light of Scripture and tradition, and this reflection forms the basis for *praxis*, that is, action that promotes social justice and particularly the liberation of the poor. The book has three main parts. The first explores the deficiencies of much classic spirituality (particularly its elitism and tendency to excessive interiority) and the new form of spirituality that came into existence in Latin America. The second part of the book describes the fundamentals of all Christian spirituality (understood as discipleship, following Jesus), and the final part of the book outlines five key features of a spirituality of liberation: conversion and solidarity, gratuitousness and efficacious love, joy (which also includes the themes of martyrdom and victory over suffering), spiritual childhood (which implies commitment to the poor), and finally community—that spirituality is a spirituality *of a people* rather than of individuals in isolation.

Another of Gutiérrez's books relevant to prophetic spirituality is *On Job: God-Talk and the Suffering of the Innocent*. This has been described as a breakthrough in his theology.[40] Gutiérrez's interpretation of Job underlines clearly that prayer and contemplation are paramount in his approach to the connections between theology and social engagement. In his interpretation of the book of Job, the difference between Job and his friends is that the latter base their reflections on abstract principles rather than on an encounter with the limitless love and compassion of God. In contrast, Job seeks his "answers" face-to-face—one might even say head-to-head. This moves Job beyond

---

[40] See Gustavo Gutiérrez, *On Job: God-Talk and the Suffering of the Innocent* (Maryknoll, NY: Orbis Books, 1998).

purely social or ethical reasoning to spiritual reasoning—a realization that God acts out of gratuitous love. Such an insight can only arise from a kind of confrontation with God. Contemplation and confrontation are closely linked. Inevitably, this reminds us of the power of the imprecatory psalms. Job does not receive a precise answer to his questions. However, what he does receive is much deeper than what he sought. The message is that contemplation widens our perspectives. Silence, prayer, and listening to what God has to say are central to Gutiérrez's approach to social engagement. But contemplation does more. In Gutiérrez's commentary, Job's encounter with God leads him to abandon himself into God's unfathomable love, beyond abstract notions of ethics or justice. This abandonment is not the same as fatalistic acceptance. Rather, it resituates social justice within a deep sense of God's gratuitous love.

Conclusion

As this chapter has attempted to show, the Prophetic Way of spirituality is largely a product of the twentieth century. In its feminist, political, and liberationist forms, this fifth type of spirituality continues to be a powerful expression of the engagement of the Christian spiritual journey with ongoing critical social issues. In that sense, the Prophetic Way moves Christian spirituality away from an unbalanced emphasis on individualized interiority. Equally, the Prophetic Way in its global, liberationist forms represents a radical change from the previously prevailing Western Christian spiritual culture.

Conclusion:
Contemporary Practice

As I outlined in the introduction, the title of this book, *The Spiritual Way: Classic Traditions and Contemporary Practice*, emphasizes three important things in relation to Christian spirituality. First of all, spirituality is a "way." That is, it is a process, a movement, and a journey. Second, it underlines that all Christian spiritual wisdom traditions place an emphasis on growth, development, and transformation. However, while classic spiritual traditions begin with a sense of human fallibility and incompleteness, the great traditions do not promote a view of human nature as inherently flawed or evil. In their distinctive ways, the classic Christian spiritual traditions seek to lay out a pathway from a state of incompleteness toward human fullness or fulfillment. Finally, to engage with spirituality is to commit oneself to an intentional and often challenging practice of life.

In Christian theological terms, the medium for this movement toward fulfillment is God, who is classically thought of in trinitarian threefold terms as Creator, Redeemer, and Sanctifier. While God may be thought of as transcendent otherness, the Christian understanding also underlines a sense that God is intimately engaged with creation and with humanity, rather than being a distant and disengaged power figure. As Creator, God is understood to be the origin of everything, not least of human existence. Because of this, we must begin our way of understanding human identity in essentially positive terms. We are the outpouring of God's creative love. However, having said this, our lives are also a work in progress. Inevitably, we sometimes fail in our attempts to live well and to relate closely to our Creator God. Thus, when described as "Redeemer," God is also to be thought of

141

as the loving medium of healing and forgiveness. This contrasts strongly with certain approaches in the Christian past, which saw God as an angry judge whose essential action was to punish us for our sins, which were seen as demeaning God's power and glory. However, as the New Testament clearly affirms, this dimension of God as Redeemer is uniquely expressed in the life and mission of Jesus of Nazareth. While a human person in first-century Palestine, Jesus also came to be understood by the early Christians as the Christ, the Anointed One and the incarnation of God in history. Finally, to speak of God as Sanctifier, expressed in the image of God as Spirit, is to understand that God is the "within" or center of all things, including each and every one of us. In other words, God is the active positive power at the heart of all our lives.

As we saw in chapter 1, the scriptural foundations of Christian spirituality are clear that the center of an authentic spiritual life is "discipleship," which is to follow the way of Jesus. Importantly, this concept of discipleship and its ideals applies to every Christian without exception and has nothing to do with privileged status. It is my hope that when we return in our contemporary times to this rich scriptural concept, it will help to underline strongly that our approach to Christian spirituality should be egalitarian and nonhierarchical. This obviously contrasts strongly with many inherited attitudes to the spiritual way that go back hundreds of years. These attitudes tended to give priority to specialized spiritual groups, such as the clergy or members of religious orders. Such people were a privileged class who were able to live out a true "spirituality" because they had stepped aside from the everyday world. As a consequence, the vast majority of ordinary Christians were limited to the practice of "devotions."

This book has attempted to show that spirituality in a Christian context has appeared throughout history via a rich range of classic traditions, each with a distinctive approach to spiritual wisdom. However, none of these inherited traditions is a self-contained or fully complete package. What is passed on to succeeding generations is then further developed and enriched in each new context (of both time and place) within which it is received and practiced. Finally, the notion of Christian spirituality as a family of classic traditions also implies that spirituality involves *shared* wisdom within a community of belief and practice rather than being something that is purely individualistic.

Contemporary Challenges

I want to conclude this book with a few reflections about how my five chosen types of classic Christian spirituality may engage with contemporary situations and concerns. However, before returning to the different types, I need to outline how I understand our contemporary world. My response obviously reflects my particular context. How each of us understands critical contemporary issues will not look precisely the same in Africa, for example, as it does in North America. Equally, what we highlight at this moment as important contemporary concerns will have changed in twenty years' time. In terms of my own perspectives, over the years I have studied and worked in a number of countries and continents, been exposed to a range of cultures and religious traditions, and been actively engaged in interreligious dialogue. However, while these experiences have enriched me in significant ways, I cannot escape my own background as British, European, and Roman Catholic Christian, shaped by values that arose from the Second Vatican Council.

Many Western thinkers these days suggest that we exist in what they call a postmodern world, where the simple answers and optimism of a previous age are no longer viable. Postmodernity rejects an unquestioning confidence in an ordered view of the world and the power of human reason to consistently come up with answers.[1] One effect of this cultural change during the latter part of the twentieth century is that people are suspicious of normative frameworks of "truth," including those associated with organized religion. As a result, in Western countries active membership of the Christian church has noticeably declined, along with a wider loss of trust in conventional authority structures. Equally, the previously dominant thought patterns of old-style liberalism are in decline and so its values and assumptions can no longer be taken for granted in the political

---

[1] For brief overviews of the culture of postmodernity, see Sheldrake, *Spirituality: A Brief History*, 174–75, and Philip Sheldrake, *Explorations in Spirituality: History, Theology and Social Practice* (Mahwah, NJ: Paulist Press, 2010), 54–55.

world or in wider society. In Europe and North America we also face the rise of what is now called the New Right—even of neofascist and neo-Nazi groups. Increasingly, we hear the language of nationalistic populism, of racism, of the return of anti-Semitism, and of violent confrontation with otherness. This is a profoundly disturbing and challenging phenomenon.

Apart from these political and structural issues, the contemporary Western world is prone to a range of other cultural and social challenges. In my judgment these include a society that is increasingly anxious, unstable, and uncertain. Also, people's lives are too often dominated by the values of contemporary consumerism ("I have, therefore I am"), a tendency to be excessively individualistic, and a desire for dogmatic certainty. Paradoxically, this quest for certainty sits alongside the decline in conventional religions and a loss of faith in the authority of traditional social and political establishments. Individualism and certainty can all too easily collapse into egotism and narcissism.

The Quest for Spirituality

However, in a striking contrast to such self-enclosed attitudes, the number of people who seek a more aspirational approach to life outside the boundaries of conventional religion is increasing. This moves people beyond "I want to be successful or wealthy" toward a desire to live with greater meaning and to conduct life in the best possible way. How can our human spirit achieve its full potential? How can we practice a holistic, integrated approach to life? If being happy is a value, what does true "happiness" really mean? How are we to thrive? As already noted in chapter 1, this quest for a more self-reflective life rather than an unexamined life has led to an increasing interest in the notion of spirituality, in both personal and professional worlds. In this context, the riches of the traditions of Christian spirituality have much to offer in response to a range of challenging issues in what could be described as an age of disruption and fragmentation.[2]

---

[2] I have attempted to describe and reflect upon the contemporary broad use of the notion of spirituality in two short books: *Spirituality: A Very Short Introduction* (Oxford: Oxford University Press, 2012), and *Spirituality: A Guide for the Perplexed* (London: Bloomsbury, 2014).

More broadly, there are some interesting contemporary instances of how the notion of spirituality is being used beyond formal religion. An interesting example of the way this has been applied in the world of education is the concept of spiritual development in documentation for English secondary (that is, high) schools produced by the UK government Office for Standards in Education (Ofsted) in 2004. Here, *spirituality* is defined as "the development of the non-material element of a human being, which animates and sustains us." The purpose of including spirituality in the school curriculum is "about the development of a sense of identity, self-worth, personal insight, meaning and purpose. It is about the development of a pupil's 'spirit.' "[3]

Two other areas where the language of spirituality is becoming increasingly common are the fields of health care and of commerce and business. In terms of health care, there are a number of interesting centers, networks, and medical interest groups in the United States, Canada, the United Kingdom, and wider Europe. For example, in the United Kingdom there is a research project called Spirituality, Theology and Health at Durham University. Then there is a Centre for Spirituality, Health and Disability at the University of Aberdeen. In wider Europe, there is a Swiss-based European Network of Research on Religion, Spirituality and Health. Useful links are available on the website of the Center for Spirituality, Theology and Health at Duke University, North Carolina: www.spiritualityandhealth.duke.edu.

In terms of the notion of "care," spirituality offers a renewed sense of purpose and of hope. It may also suggest ways of responding to the suffering of patients for whom there is no medical cure by helping medical personnel to understand suffering as paradoxically painful and yet a way to human growth. Overall, spirituality in health care is a response to the need to move beyond a purely medicalized model of illness and care based on medication and surgery. "Health" includes a spiritual dimension. "Well-being" takes account of the totality of life, and "health" is more than simple clinical curing. Alongside the notion of holistic models of health lies the question of what constitutes "spiritual care." Spiritual care is no longer assumed to be the sole preserve of hospital chaplains but should also be a dimension of what is offered by medical personnel. Overall, spiritual care implies

[3] See Office for Standards in Education, *Promoting and Evaluating Pupils' Spiritual, Moral, Social and Cultural Development*, HMI 2125 (London: Ofsted 2004), 12.

nurturing the human spirit in those being cared for. However, it also implies something about the training and development of medical carers and what they are to offer.[4]

A second social area in which spirituality has recently appeared relates to changes in the way commercial and business life is viewed. For example, the nature of work is to be understood as a spiritual issue because it relates to questions of human purpose and meaning. Articles and books on spirituality and business studies are now quite common, and there are groups that seek to promote spiritual values in the workplace, such as the Foundation for Workplace Spirituality (www.workplacespirituality.org.uk). At the heart of this turn to spirituality in the commercial world is a recovery of the idea that work is a vocation rather than purely a practical necessity. Some companies encourage management teams to develop spiritual values and practices and organize "retreats" to build up a corporate spirit. The "business spirituality" movement also encourages the development of a clear value system as well as the importance of giving attention to the "wholeness" of the work force. Business spirituality also sometimes focuses on the qualities of leadership in the workplace. For example, the spiritually imbued leader will possess courage, creativity, and the capacity to be inspirational and thus build up team spirit and what is termed a "self-enabled" workforce. Some approaches to spiritually enlightened business leadership also include the ability to create a corporate sense of service to humanity and an ethos that suggests that part of what the business does is to seek to change the world for the better.[5]

There are also more broadly based attempts to introduce spirituality into thinking about economics and its role in society. A notable example is SPES, a European-centered international forum for Spirituality in Economics and Society.[6] The forum brings together individuals, academic centers, and values-driven organizations that are engaged in socioeconomic activity and interested in making spiritu-

---

[4] See, for example, Helen Orchard, ed., *Spirituality in Health Care Contexts* (London: Jessica Kingsley, 2001).

[5] See, for example, Robert A. Giacolone and Carole L. Jurkiewicz, eds., *Handbook of Workplace Spirituality and Organizational Performance* (Armonk, NY: Sharpe, 2003).

[6] See their website at www.eurospes.org.

ality a public and social good. SPES approaches spirituality in terms of making connections between people's quest for meaning (whether in relation to God or a broader view of the sacred) and everyday activities in the social and economic worlds. The forum explicitly seeks to promote a spiritual humanism derived partly from European personalist philosophy, to relate spirituality to a richer understanding of social ethics, and to promote hope as the key virtue in working to build a better future for Europe and the world. SPES has promoted certain key areas of research and action. Spirituality and the Economics of Frugality asks how we may reintroduce the value of frugality as a social virtue and how this might creatively impact on economics. The Spiritual Identity of Europe suggests that spirituality needs to be a key factor in rethinking the future of Europe. Finally, Globalisation and the Common Good focuses on the ancient virtue of seeking the common good and redefines it in the context of globalization, environmental problems, and the increasingly sharp socio-economic divisions in the world.

Briefly, a third contemporary example of spirituality in relation to social and public values concerns the meaning and future of cities. The related themes of spirituality and architecture, spirituality and planning, and urban spirituality have begun to make an appearance in recent times in workshops, colloquia, and publications. Examples include a book by urban planner Leonie Sandercock, *Cosmopolis II: Mongrel Cities in the 21st Century*, in which she suggests that "the spiritual" is central to the meaning and future of human cities.[7] Then, in a provocative study entitled *The City: A Global History*, Joel Kotkin writes about what makes for a successful city. Alongside other factors, Kotkin makes the point that a city is, or should be, a sacred place, embodying an inspiring vision of human existence and possibility.[8] Finally, in my book *The Spiritual City* I outline an explicitly Christian contribution to thinking about the meaning and future of cities.[9]

---

[7] Leonie Sandercock, *Cosmopolis II: Mongrel Cities in the 21st Century* (London: Continuum, 2003).

[8] Joel Kotkin, *The City: A Global History* (New York: Random House, 2006).

[9] Philip Sheldrake, *The Spiritual City: Theology, Spirituality and the Urban* (Oxford: Wiley-Blackwell, 2014).

Spirituality and Interreligious Dialogue

I now want to add a few reflections on the importance of spirituality in contemporary interreligious dialogue. This dialogue reflects an increasing global awareness within institutional Christianity, not least concerning a religiously plural world. In some parts of the world there is also an urgent need to address the close connections between religious antagonisms and violence.

The dialogue between faiths, while it involves the exploration of each other's beliefs, should not be dominated purely by theoretical discussion. In recent decades such dialogue has often developed a strongly spiritual dimension, not least in the context of contacts between Christianity and Hinduism and Christianity and Buddhism. There is a wide range of examples. As early as the 1960s, the Benedictine monk Jean-Marie Déchanet introduced many Western Christians to the purpose and techniques of yoga drawn from Hinduism and to the value of attending to the body in meditation.[10] More recently another English Benedictine monk, John Main, drew upon his earlier contacts with the Hindu guru Swami Satyananda to explore connections between the recitation of mantras and ancient Christian meditative practice derived from the writings of John Cassian. Main is best known as the inspiration behind the now well-known World Community for Christian Meditation.[11] Other Christian examples of a spiritual approach to interreligious dialogue, in this case with Zen Buddhism in Japan, include the work of Jesuits such as Hugo Enomiya-Lassalle (who became a Zen master), Kakichi Kadowaki, and William Johnston.[12]

Spirituality occupies an important place in the lives of all religious believers and therefore offers a powerful point of engagement between different faiths. Behind the institutions and structures, the heart of the different religions focuses on a process of spiritual trans-

---

[10] Jean-Marie Déchanet, *Christian Yoga* (New York: Harper & Brothers, 1960).

[11] See, for example, John Main, *Word into Silence: A Manual for Christian Meditation*, new ed. (Norwich, UK: Canterbury Press, 2006).

[12] See, for example, Hugo Enomiya-Lassalle, *The Practice of Zen Meditation* (London: Thorsons, 1990); Kakichi Kadowaki, *Zen and the Bible* (Maryknoll, NY: Orbis Books, 2002); and William Johnston, *The Still Point: Reflections on Zen and Christian Mysticism* (New York: Fordham University Press, 1989).

formation. Those of us with experience of interreligious encounter have come to realize that a quest to share spiritual wisdom may lead us to new ways of self-understanding and helps to create a spiritual common ground. This does not make differences of belief disappear, but it helps to shift our perceptions about the key theoretical distinctions between the religions.

Christian Spiritual Wisdom—The Way of Discipline

In the light of these and other contemporary spiritual challenges, what might my five chosen types of Christian spiritual wisdom offer by way of response? Apart from suggesting the way they may encourage changes in our mentality and values, I will briefly suggest a few spiritual practices that may assist these changes. Spiritual practices in an authentic sense are more than simply devotional or relaxing exercises. They are regular, disciplined activities that both express a particular vision of life and seek to consolidate this through a framework of meditative action.

The first type, the Way of Discipline, offers a range of critical values that counter some prevailing social dysfunctions, especially in the Western world. The notion of discipline has historically been associated with the language of asceticism (*askēsis*—that is, focused training). Asceticism has powerful things to say in reaction to consumerism and materialism and against a contemporary desire for everything to be easily, immediately, and completely available to us. Equally, the notion of discipline counteracts the dangers of an unfocused and fragmented existence by promoting a well-ordered life with a sense of purpose and direction. Such purpose and direction depend on being able increasingly to identify our deepest life-giving desires as opposed to our more superficial and immediate wants and then becoming capable of living in the light of this deep desire. The notion of self-denial can sound highly negative and punitive, but, understood correctly, it has a more positive meaning. In the best sense, self-denial is not self-punishment but involves a healthy awareness of disorder and a lack of balance in our lives and of our need to be freed from unhelpful dependencies.

In the face of an ecological crisis, provoked in part by human greed as well as the culture of consumerism, there are clearly immediate and important reasons for promoting the value of *askēsis*. Among other things, the Way of Discipline speaks of the value of trying to create a pattern of regularity and rhythm in our daily lives. It also suggests that we should value periodic abstention from excess—for example, too much eating, drinking, or shopping. We may also find it helpful to step aside regularly from our normal life patterns, particularly fragmented or over-busy ones, to focus for short periods of time on a spiritual practice that may help us to become recentered and also to identify habits that are unhealthy or in some way entrap us. Examples of popular spiritual practices are yoga, tai chi, and a pattern of focused meditation such as mindfulness meditation or Zen meditation. The fact that some increasingly popular spiritual practices draw upon other world religions, such as Buddhism, should not deter us. Some people also find it helpful occasionally to step aside from normal life patterns for a longer period of retreat in a place where there is both solitude and the availability of an accompanying spiritual guide. This modern equivalent of the desert might be a spirituality center in the midst of a city or a literal wilderness in a remote rural retreat house that also brings us close to the purifying power of nature in woods, hills, or the ocean.

It is also worth remembering that the Way of Discipline, expressed, for example, in classic monasticism, also promotes social values beyond a purely individualized understanding of asceticism. There is the monastic teaching on silence as a way of learning to listen to others with care and attentiveness plus "restraint of speech"—in other words, refraining from destructive gossip or from being assertive or domineering. Of course, as we appreciate strongly these days, we also need to avoid the wrong kind of silence. By that I mean a silence that is an expression not of attentiveness but rather the opposite. This false silence involves a failure to speak out in the face of abuse, prejudice, persecution, injustice, and wrongdoing. The classic monastic rules also, in a variety of ways, suggest challenging ways of building human community. In a Western world of increasing diversity and fear of otherness, the robust teaching on hospitality to the stranger in the Rule of St. Benedict or on working for the common good in the Rule of St. Augustine is challenging and provocative. These are much-needed spiritual values, particularly in today's multicultural, densely populated, and often conflicted global cities. There has been a loss of neighborliness and a sense of solidarity or mutual care that desperately needs to be restored for the common good.

The spiritual practice known as *lectio divina* has historically been associated with the Way of Discipline, and particularly with monastic life. In recent years it has become popular with a much wider Christian public. *Lectio divina* is intended to be a way of entering more deeply and personally into the words of Scripture and, from that starting point, moving to a close personal presence to God. Over time, this has the capacity to transform our consciousness and our way of being. As noted in chapter 2, this ancient practice was given a more structured framework of four dimensions or stages in the Middle Ages. The basis was a deep desire to encounter God and to be transformed through that encounter. The first stage, *lectio*, literally means "reading." However, in practical terms, what Scripture are we to read for meditative purposes? If possible, it makes sense to select a short passage that speaks to the reader's situation or is particularly provocative or challenging. If no scriptural phrase or passage immediately comes to mind, three suggestions occur to me. First, Psalm 139, in verses 1 to 18, meditates powerfully on God's nearness and intimacy with us. Then there are the fundamental teachings of Jesus embodied in the nine blessings or Beatitudes in the Sermon on the Mount (Matthew 5). Finally, Jesus' parable of the Good Samaritan in the Gospel of Luke, chapter 10 (in response to the question "Who is my neighbor?") has challenging things to say about who we are to think of as neighbors and how we are to respond to strangers. Ancient practice implied not simply reading a scripture text with the eyes but also pronouncing the words quietly with the lips. Anyone who has undertaken this practice will know that such quiet mouthing of Scripture has a particular power.

The second stage of *lectio divina* is *meditatio*—literally "meditation." This may embrace a range of elements, such as reflection on the Scripture passage or the repetition of a few chosen words or phrases that have a particular power. This "rumination" on or chewing over of the words is in order that they be digested and in some way embedded in our heart. Importantly, this stage has no fixed timespan. Ultimately, this meditation, if it touches our inner spirit, will lead us toward the third stage, *oratio*. This literally means "prayer," but it fundamentally implies a heartfelt and spontaneous conversation with

God. Again, this may be brief or extended. The final stage of *lectio* is called *contemplatio*, which is translated as "contemplation." This does not necessarily mean being drawn into an elevated spiritual state. Rather, our deep conversation with God is likely to lead us ultimately into a space where words will cease. In that space I simply remain still in an immediacy of presence to God.[13]

The Contemplative-Mystical Way

As I made clear in chapter 3, my second type of spiritual wisdom, the Contemplative-Mystical Way, is not to be understood as esoteric, withdrawn from the everyday, or concerned merely with a self-focused interiority. There is a strong fascination with mysticism these days. The word appears to promise special insights, deep wisdom, or even the key to the meaning of life. The notion of mysticism generally points to the idea that we can have an intimate encounter with, and perhaps some inner knowledge of, the mystery of God. In other words, mysticism implies a kind of direct and personal *experience* in contrast to the way people usually think about religion—as buildings, institutional structures, rituals, doctrines, and rules. Indeed, mysticism, like the other popular word *spirituality*, is sometimes contrasted favorably with *religion* in this institutional sense. Some people see mysticism as the essence of all true religion that lies behind the different belief languages we use. They see the mystical as a common stream running through the great religions, from Roman Catholic Christianity to Tibetan Buddhism, in a way that is not ultimately dependent on their differences.

Why is mysticism so popular? I think that there are two main and closely related reasons. Both have to do with what I think of as the crises of our modern age and the resulting intense human needs. First, many people want to transcend the boundaries that characterize their normal worlds and experience unity with other people or harmony with nature. They wish to overcome the divisions within humanity, whether these are political, religious, social, or cultural, and

---

[13] For a modern study of *lectio divina*, see Michael Casey, *Sacred Reading: The Ancient Art of Lectio Divina* (Ligouri, MO: Triumph Books, 1996).

also humanity's alienation from wider nature. This is because people experience these divisions as deeply destructive. As a result, people look for something in common on a deeper spiritual level. However, because organized religion is too often riddled with mutual suspicion, people look for spiritual contexts that bypass these unattractive realities. Second, a variety of social, economic, and political factors make many people dissatisfied with the ability of purely material enhancement to fulfill human aspirations. Thus, the current crisis of meaning, fears for the future of humanity, and a certain cynicism about humanly created authority structures (both political and in the church) may be overcome by accessing a level of consciousness that is available *intuitively* rather than by purely intellectual means. Mysticism therefore seems to offer a connection with the mysterious depths of human existence.

The Contemplative-Mystical Way offers a sense of holism, of the interconnectedness of life, as well as opening up connections to "the more" and potentially to "the all." It is also a way of knowing beyond the purely rational. It fosters attentiveness or what Buddhism would call mindfulness. The Contemplative-Mystical Way also emphasizes "being present" in the fullest sense—and staying in place—rather than skipping around from one thing to another or simply dipping our toes into situations, events, and life. At the heart of being present is the cultivation of an immediacy of presence to the absolute. Importantly, while in the Christian way of understanding the absolute, God, is love and healing, God also demands a generous response to love. This is to be shown via an equally generous response to people, not least to the stranger, and to the endangered world of wider creation. This contemplative-mystical approach to presence and to a generosity of response also counters any tendency to see feeling good and happy as an end in itself. The aim of the Contemplative-Mystical Way is to draw us beyond the immediate to the never ending. It implies a transfiguration of the ordinary and being made one with the depths of ourselves, with others, and with ultimacy—that is, God. In this way, everyday reality is transformed into something wondrous.

At the heart of a Christian approach to the Contemplative-Mystical Way is desire—a certain kind of intense longing that moves us ever onward. We are driven by what it is we do not yet fully know or finally possess. The mystical way turns the spiritual seeker into a perpetual wanderer. In the words of the French Jesuit Michel de Certeau, an outstanding scholar of mysticism, "He or she is a mystic who cannot stop walking and, with the certainty of what is lacking, knows of every place and object that it is *not that*; one cannot stay *there* nor be content with *that*. Desire creates an excess. Places are exceeded, passed, lost behind it. It makes one go further, elsewhere. It lives nowhere."[14]

As we saw in chapter 3, in the Christian contemplative-mystical tradition there has been an important emphasis that contemplation should never be separated from ethical behavior (for example, the writings of John Ruusbroec). More radically, the Chilean theologian Segundo Galilea wrote a great deal concerning the vital mystical or contemplative dimensions of responses to injustice. Social engagement must be accompanied by a process of interior transformation. This is the heart of what he called "integral liberation."[15] Galilea promoted a reformulation of the idea of contemplation and of the mystical. At the heart of the Christian tradition, he suggests, has always been the notion of contemplation as a supreme act of self-forgetfulness rather than a preoccupation with personal interiority. In the teachings of the great mystics, contemplation has always been related to the classic Christian themes of cross and death.

> This implies the crucifixion of egoism and the purification of the self as a condition of contemplation. This crucifixion of egoism in forgetfulness of self in the dialectic prayer-commitment will be brought to fulfilment both in the mystical dimension of communication with Jesus in the luminous night of faith, and also in the sacrifice which is assumed by commitment to the liberation of others. The "death" of mysticism and the "death" of the militant are the two dimensions of the call to accept the cross, as the condition of being a disciple. . . . The desert as a political experience liberates [the Christian] from egoism and from the "system," and is a source of freedom and of an ability to liberate.[16]

[14] De Certeau, *The Mystic Fable*, 299.
[15] Segundo Galilea, "The Spirituality of Liberation," 186–94.
[16] Segundo Galilea, "Liberation as an Encounter with Politics and Contemplation," 535–36.

What Christian spiritual practices fit with this Contemplative-Mystical Way? There is a range of meditative approaches that promote a process of centering that leads to inner stillness (*hesychia*). This is also related to self-forgetfulness and to spiritual transformation. The most ancient form is the Eastern Christian practice known as the Jesus Prayer, or the Prayer of the Name, which traces its origins to early desert monasticism. The prayer amounts to a slow and sustained repetition of the phrase "Lord Jesus Christ, Son of God, have mercy on me a sinner," which may be shortened to "Lord Jesus have mercy" (but not usually the name *Jesus* on its own). The recitation should be slow and linked to the rhythm of our breathing. The Jesus Prayer may be used as a formal exercise or it may more informally accompany our daily work. This is what the early desert fathers and mothers thought of as continuous prayer. Either way, this spiritual practice is not to be understood mechanically but involves a deep inner transformation. It therefore demands careful spiritual guidance.[17]

Returning to the process of "centering," there is also a modern method of Christian meditation known precisely as centering prayer, associated with monastic writers such as the Cistercian Thomas Keating and the Benedictine John Main but intended for a wider public.[18] This practice bears a close resemblance to the Jesus Prayer tradition and also to the practice of mantra meditation in Hinduism. Certain practical steps are suggested. Sit comfortably, relax, close your eyes, and seek to quieten yourself. Then, choose a sacred word that supports your desire to be present to God and open to God's action. Focus your mind on this word and let it be present to you. Finally, whenever you are aware of thoughts or images or feelings that intrude, simply return your mind to the sacred word.

Finally, in the *Spiritual Exercises* of Ignatius Loyola, there is an often-overlooked appendix that outlines "three ways of prayer." The third way is "by rhythm" or "the prayer of the breath." This

---

[17] See, for example, Pentkovsky, *The Pilgrim's Tale*, and John Anthony McGuckin, "Jesus Prayer," in *The New SCM Dictionary of Christian Spirituality*, ed. Philip Sheldrake.

[18] See, for example, Thomas Keating, *Open Mind, Open Heart: The Contemplative Dimension of the Gospel* (New York: Continuum, 1998); and John Main, *Essential Writings* (Maryknoll, NY: Orbis Books, 2002).

suggests a slow, rhythmic recitation of a familiar prayer, such as the Our Father, with each word in turn linked to our breathing—a single word in the interval between each breath. This approach is most unusual in Western Christian spirituality, and there has been some speculation about where Ignatius Loyola discovered it. Some commentators think that it may echo Eastern Christian hesychastic practices. The difficulty with this idea is to know how and when Ignatius Loyola would have encountered these practices. More controversially, there is a credible suggestion that the influence on Ignatius was the prayer of the breath in the Al-Andalus Sufi tradition (arguably itself partly derived from Eastern Christianity) that would have still been known in late-medieval Spain.

The Way of Practical Action

The reference to Ignatius Loyola brings me naturally to the third type of spirituality, the Way of Practical Action. This approach to Christian spirituality promotes attentiveness to everyday reality and how to enter more deeply into this reality beyond the surface of things. This awareness of, and responsiveness to, the external world around us embraces threats to the physical environment as well as people's individual needs and the critical situations within wider society. As the title suggests, this is a spirituality of engagement and action as opposed to detachment and passivity. It also promotes the practical as opposed to abstract theory or spiritualized interiority. As a spiritual path, the Way of Practical Action espouses the spiritual importance of moral virtue and ethical behavior. Examples would include acceptance of others, forgiveness, compassion, tolerance, charity, a sense of social responsibility, freedom from egoism (what Ignatius Loyola characterizes as "humility" in the fullest sense), and disinterested service. We are to become people *for* others and people genuinely *alongside* others. Such a focus on service responds to actual human needs and also counters an unfortunate human tendency to be self-seeking. This type of spirituality also invites us to reevaluate the everyday and the ordinary. It involves becoming intentionally embedded in daily life as a doorway to the transcendent. Theologically, it affirms that the ordinary is filled with the divine. Nothing is too little, nothing is too low, nothing is without spiritual value.

In the thinking of Ignatius Loyola, to reach this level of spiritual engagement with everyday life demands that we seek to become free from what he calls "disordered attachments" in order to be able to respond wholeheartedly to the call of Christ to share in the mission of God in the world. As I outlined in chapter 4, a critical aspect of Ignatian spirituality enables us to enter effectively into the Way of Practical Action developing a capacity for discernment—that is, learning how to distinguish between what is life-giving and what is disordered or destructive and then acting in the light of this insight.

To be of value today, this Way of Practical Action needs to touch upon the challenging needs of our contemporary society. How can we rebuild neighborliness on our streets? In an increasingly multicultural world, how can we respond creatively to otherness and to strangers? How can we recover a sense of service (as opposed to efficient mechanics) in the social professions, such as teaching, health care, social work, and policing—not to mention among politicians and people working in the financial sector? Also, in what sense are local services, such as transport or care of the streets (cleaning and repairing), a social *right* and part of sustaining community, rather than a gratuitous gift by local government that may be cut or withdrawn?

Finally, to nurture the Way of Practical Action, what might be a helpful spiritual practice? In the *Spiritual Exercises* of Ignatius Loyola there is a daily spiritual practice known as the Examen. This was conventionally described as an "examination of conscience" with strong moral overtones and associated largely with eliminating our faults and personal sins. This approach was somewhat mechanistic and focused only on fault-finding. However, in recent decades and in the light of a renewed emphasis in the Ignatian spiritual tradition on effective practical action in the everyday world, the Examen has been creatively reread. It is now regularly described as an Examen (or examination) of *Consciousness*.[19] This then becomes a daily spiritual practice of focused attention on where God has been "speaking" to us in ordinary events or human encounters during the day and

[19] See, for example, George Aschenbrenner, "Consciousness Examen," *Review for Religious* 31 (1972): 14–21.

how we have responded or failed to respond. As a spiritual practice, the Examen of Consciousness is an action of discernment. Nowadays it is sometimes described as having five stages or dimensions. The first stage is to become aware of God's presence and to ask God for enlightenment—that is, insight that enables us to see our life as God sees it. The second stage is to turn our attention specifically to the day that has just ended and thank God for all the gifts that God has given us in that day. In this context, we may recall the events that happened and people we have met. The third stage is then to become aware of our feelings during the day, not least our struggles and fears. Where do we now feel that we failed to respond fully to God's gifts and action in our lives? The fourth stage is to focus on one important feeling, event, or action during the day. This may also be where we need to change and become more responsive, including repentance for our failures to be properly aware of God's action in the day or to be generous in our response. The fifth and final stage is to look ahead to the next day. Here we express our desire to respond to God in the events of the coming day and to ask for guidance so that we may be aware of God speaking to us in the midst of the everyday and be able to respond generously

The Way of Beauty

In chapter 5 I suggested that the Way of Beauty was a less familiar approach to the spiritual journey. However, in this approach, aesthetics is to be understood as rich in spiritual potential, whether through the medium of nature, art, music, or poetry. In our contemporary context, this way invites us to go beyond superficial understandings of beauty as a source of pleasure or satisfaction, as in the manufacture of "beauty products" or comments such as "Our new car is a real beauty" or "You're looking really beautiful today." The beautiful and aesthetic is more than merely decorative, colorful, stylish, or well-designed. These are very utilitarian understandings of beauty. Philosophically and theologically, beauty has been understood as an important human value, linked to virtue and to the sublime. As the medieval Franciscan theologian John Duns Scotus and the seventeenth-century Anglican writer Thomas Traherne remind us, ultimate beauty is a characteristic of God's being and yet is reflected in the least created thing. The great medieval cathedrals, with their purposeful design, also associate beauty with order and harmony. Beauty perceived through nature, art, music, and poetry acts upon the human spirit and enriches our sensibility, sight, and hearing and affects our mood, beliefs, and attitudes to life.

What forms of spiritual practice might help to deepen the Way of Beauty in our lives? Perhaps more than any other spiritual way, this is very dependent on individual sensibilities. In relation to my own experience of nature, I can be especially transformed—indeed, transported to another place—by simply watching the ocean while sitting on a cliff top or walking along an isolated beach. In terms of humanly created beauty, I have already noted how reading the religious poetry of George Herbert provoked a quasi-mystical experience in the French Jewish philosopher Simone Weil. For many people, quietly reading poetry has a transformative effect. The same applies to music, especially music that is overtly spiritual or stylistically evocative rather than rambunctious. I recall being very surprised many years ago, while at a drinks reception, when someone mentioned the powerful effect of listening to recordings of monastic Gregorian chant at the end of a busy day. Equally surprising was how many other people in the group (mostly nonreligious people) echoed this experience!

Finally, while discussing the interplay of beauty and meaning in medieval religious buildings, I noted that the majority of people today who enter such churches have little or no understanding of their original symbolism or spiritual meaning. However, this does not result in the complete abandonment of ancient churches as spiritual space by the nonreligious majority of visitors. In fact, contemporary research suggests that the majority of visitors to the great medieval cathedrals do not view them simply as museums or historical monuments. There is a residual sense of the sacred even in an increasingly post-religious Western culture that actually attracts people into such buildings in order to find some sense of the sacred and some spiritual experience.[20] Most of the great medieval churches in my country explicitly offer quiet spaces for reflection or meditation. To sit quietly in these spaces, or even to sit in the main body of the church, can be

---

[20] See Grace Davie, *Religion in Modern Europe: A Memory Mutates* (Oxford: Oxford University Press, 2000), 164.

a powerful spiritual practice as we allow the power of the architecture and the evocative mixture of intimate spaces and vast space, as well as the play of light on the stone, to speak to us.

The Prophetic Way

Finally, what of the Prophetic Way? This approach to spirituality is very much a product of our own times. It invites us to critique and radically question established ways of thinking, behaving, and constructing our contexts—whether the street, the neighborhood, or society in general. From the Scriptures onward, prophetic figures were and are disturbing voices that robustly tell us the way the world really is in contrast to the way we prefer to think it is. Prophetic voices therefore point us beyond the apparently "fixed" and "established" toward something new that may be creative and restorative, but is also profoundly challenging. The quest for human justice and equality of all kinds, not to mention a confrontation with global ecological destruction, will demand that all of us seriously change our lives.

If we are to think of the Prophetic Way as a spiritual path, what might this mean in terms of spiritual practice? First of all, it will imply a rather different way of understanding the process of being present to God and conversing with God. For example, what the monastic practice of *lectio divina* refers to as *oratio* and what Ignatian spirituality calls a colloquy—the conclusion to a time of meditation—implies "conversation." But conversation with God should not be thought of as purely intimate, comfortable, and comforting. Such conversation may be robust in both directions. Political theologian Johann Baptist Metz noted that prayer is a limitless language with no barriers. Everything can, and should, be said to God in prayer, including our frustration and anger.[21] In a similar way, in his book *On Job*, Gustavo Gutiérrez not only underlines how prayer and contemplation are central to his theology of liberation but also, in describing how Job actively *confronts* God, draws out the close links between contemplation, confrontation, and liberation. Yet, in and through this confronta-

---

[21] See the comments on Metz's approach to prayer by Martinez, *Confronting the Mystery of God*, 87.

tion Job is led to experience God's loving and redeeming "answer" beyond abstract notions of justice. Having said this, Job's robust conversation with God forces him to change his perspectives. In general, conversation as a spiritual practice risks encountering a God who also challenges us in radical and demanding ways to see differently, to act differently, and to be in the world differently.

This notion of colloquy or conversation applies not merely to our engagement with God but also to our human practices. So, in terms of the Prophetic Way, a challenging question is with whom, or with what kinds of people, are we ready to have a conversation? Is it only with people like ourselves or of whom we approve? Or do we consciously engage with otherness, the stranger? Not least, I am thinking of those—such as people who are homeless—who are effectively without a social identity and who do not merit recognition by the majority of the people who pass by. In this context, to enter into conversation with those who are marginalized is, in modest ways, a prophetic act. It both recognizes their equality with us and may also, in some way, help to re-empower them by acknowledging not only that they exist but also that they have viewpoints about life that need to be heard and responded to.

More substantially, beyond this notion of transforming conversation, some of us may seek to become more deeply involved with people marginalized by mainstream society by volunteering at local emergency or housing shelters, or in drop-in centers for people who, although they are housed, are nevertheless so financially challenged that they have to rely on food banks for their meals. For many people who have become involved with such work—for example, as volunteers in the houses of hospitality run by the Catholic Worker Movement—this is not merely a matter of work for social justice but is a genuine spiritual practice to which they commit themselves. Such practice has the potential to transform their consciousness, their values, and their way of being a presence in the everyday world. Interestingly, the origin of the word *conversation* in Old English has implications of commitment—living with, familiarity with, and intimacy. This looks back to the Latin word *conversatio*, which has implications of a common way of life followed with conviction rather than merely an exchange of words.

Concluding Thoughts

All of my five chosen types of spiritual wisdom and practice offer radical and transformative possibilities for contemporary spiritual seekers. While the examples I have suggested are overtly Christian, my experience and belief are that, properly understood, their wisdom is accessible and meaningful to a wider audience. The types of spirituality do not merely encourage spiritual practices in a narrow sense. They also identify human-spiritual values, linked to the vision of an ethical life. This will undoubtedly challenge us but has the potential to identify what is humanly disordered and to offer a path toward inner freedom and a transforming encounter with the sacred and the transcendent.

Selected Readings

Aschenbrenner, George. "Consciousness Examen." *Review for Religious* 31 (1972): 14–21.

Balasuriya, Tissa. *Mary and Human Liberation: The Story and the Text*. Harrisburg, PA: Trinity, 1997.

Berleant, Arnold. *The Aesthetics of Environment*. Philadelphia: Temple University Press, 1992.

Boesak, Alan. *Farewell to Innocence: A Socio-Ethical Study on Black Theology and Power*. Maryknoll, NY: Orbis Books, 1978.

Boff, Leonardo. "The Need for Political Saints: From a Spirituality of Liberation to the Practice of Liberation." *Cross Currents* 30, no. 4 (Winter 1980–81): 369–84.

———. *Saint Francis: A Model of Human Liberation*. London: SCM Press, 1982.

Bonhoeffer, Dietrich. *The Cost of Discipleship*. New York: Touchstone, 1995.

———. *Letters and Papers from Prison*. New York: Touchstone, 1997.

Brown, Peter. *The Body and Society: Men, Women and Sexual Renunciation in Early Christianity*. London: Faber & Faber, 1991.

———. *The Making of Late Antiquity*. Cambridge, MA: Harvard University Press, 1993.

Burton-Christie, Douglas. *The Word in the Desert*. Oxford: Oxford University Press, 1993.

Bynum, Caroline Walker. *Jesus as Mother: Studies in the Spirituality of the High Middle Ages*. Berkeley: University of California Press, 1984.

Camille, Michael. *Gothic Art: Visions and Revelations of the Medieval World*. London: Weidenfeld & Nicolson, 1996.

Carrette, Jeremy, and Richard King. *Selling Spirituality: The Silent Takeover of Religion*. London: Routledge, 2004.

Casaldáliga, Pedro, and José-María Vigil. *Political Holiness: A Spirituality of Liberation*. Maryknoll, NY: Orbis Books, 1994.

Casey, Michael. *Sacred Reading: The Ancient Art of Lectio Divina*. Ligouri, MO: Triumph Books, 1996.

Chase, Steven. *Contemplation and Compassion: The Victorine Tradition*. London: Darton, Longman & Todd, 2003.

Chryssavgis, John. *Light through Darkness: The Orthodox Tradition*. London: Darton, Longman & Todd, 2004.

Colledge, Edmund, and James Walsh, trans. *Guigo II: Ladder of Monks and Twelve Meditations*. Collegeville, MN: Cistercian Publications, 1981.

———, trans. *Julian of Norwich: Showings*. Classics of Western Spirituality. Mahwah, NJ: Paulist Press, 1978.

Countryman, William. *The Poetic Imagination: An Anglican Spiritual Tradition*. London: Darton, Longman & Todd, 1999.

Cousins, Ewert, trans. *Bonaventure: The Soul's Journey into God, The Tree of Life, The Life of St. Francis*. Classics of Western Spirituality. Mahwah, NJ: Paulist Press, 1978.

Cunningham, Lawrence S. *Thomas Merton and the Monastic Vision*. Grand Rapids, MI: Eerdmans, 1999.

———, ed. *Thomas Merton: Spiritual Master. The Essential Writings*. Mahwah, NJ: Paulist Press, 1992.

Cunningham, Lawrence S., and Keith J. Egan. *Christian Spirituality: Themes from the Tradition*. Mahwah, NJ: Paulist Press, 1996.

De Catanzaro, C. J. trans. *Symeon the New Theologian: The Discourses*. Classics of Western Spirituality. Mahwah, NJ: Paulist Press, 1980.

De Caussade, Jean-Pierre. *Abandonment to Divine Providence*. New York: Doubleday Image Books, 1975.

De Certeau, Michel. "Culture and Spiritual Experience." *Concilium* 19 (1966): 331.

———. "How is Christianity Thinkable Today?" In *The Postmodern God*, ed. Graham Ward. Oxford: Blackwell, 1997.

———. *The Mystic Fable*. Volume 1. Chicago: University of Chicago Press, 1992.

Déchanet, Jean-Marie. *Christian Yoga*. New York: Harper & Brothers, 1960.

De Gruchy, John W. *Reconciliation: Restoring Justice*. London: SCM Press, 2002.

De Sales, Francis. *Introduction to the Devout Life*. New York: Doubleday, 1982.

De Waal, Esther. *Seeking God: The Way of St. Benedict.* Collegeville, MN: Liturgical Press, 1984.

Duby, Georges. *The Age of the Cathedral: Art and Society 980–1420.* Chicago: University of Chicago Press, 1981.

Eco, Umberto. *Art and Beauty in the Middle Ages.* New Haven, CT: Yale University Press, 1986.

Ellacuría, Ignacio, and Jon Sobrino, eds. *Mysterium Liberationis: Fundamental Concepts of Liberation Theology.* Maryknoll, NY: Orbis Books, 1993.

Ellsberg, Robert, ed. *Charles de Foucauld: Selected Writings.* Maryknoll, NY: Orbis Books, 1999.

———. *Dorothy Day: Selected Writings.* Maryknoll, NY: Orbis Books, 1992.

Enomiya-Lassalle, Hugo. *The Practice of Zen Meditation.* London: Thorsons, 1990.

Espin, Orlando O., and Gary Macy, eds. *Futuring our Past: Explorations in the Theology of Tradition.* Maryknoll, NY: Orbis Books, 2006.

Evans, G. R., trans. *Bernard of Clairvaux: Selected Works.* Classics of Western Spirituality. Mahwah, NJ: Paulist Press, 1987.

Fedotov, G. P., ed. *A Treasury of Russian Spirituality.* London: Sheed & Ward, 1981.

Ferguson, Everett, and Abraham J. Malherbe, trans. and eds. *Gregory of Nyssa: The Life of Moses.* Classics of Western Spirituality. Mahwah, NJ: Paulist Press, 1978.

Flanagan, Kieran, and Peter Jupp, eds. *A Sociology of Spirituality.* Aldershot, UK: Ashgate, 2007.

Galilea, Segundo. "Liberation as an Encounter with Politics and Contemplation." In *Understanding Mysticism*, ed. Richard Woods, 535–36. London: Athlone Press, 1980.

———. "The Spirituality of Liberation." *The Way* (July 1985): 186–94.

Giacolone, Robert A., and Carole L. Jurkiewicz, eds. *Handbook of Workplace Spirituality and Organizational Performance.* Armonk, NY: Sharpe, 2003.

Greer, Rowan A., trans. and ed. *Origen.* Classics of Western Spirituality. Mahwah, NJ: Paulist Press, 1979.

Gregg, Robert C., ed. *Athanasius: The Life of Anthony.* Mahwah, NJ: Paulist Press, 1980.

Gutiérrez, Gustavo. *On Job: God-Talk and the Suffering of the Innocent*, Maryknoll, NY: Orbis Books, 1998.

————. *We Drink from Our Own Wells: The Spiritual Journey of a People.* Maryknoll, NY: Orbis Books, 1984.

Hall, Bill, and David Jasper, eds. *Art and the Spiritual.* Sunderland, UK: University of Sunderland Press, 2003.

Harmless, William. *Desert Christians: An Introduction to the Literature of Early Monasticism.* Oxford: Oxford University Press, 2004.

Hart, Columba, trans. *Hadewijch: The Complete Works.* Classics of Western Spirituality. Mahwah, NJ: Paulist Press, 1980.

Hausherr, Irénée. *Spiritual Direction in the Early Christian East.* Kalamazoo, MI: Cistercian Publications, 1990.

Heelas, Paul, and Linda Woodhead. *The Spiritual Revolution: Why Religion is Giving Way to Spirituality.* Oxford: Wiley-Blackwell, 2005.

Himes, Kenneth. *Modern Catholic Social Teaching: Commentaries and Interpretations.* Washington, DC: Georgetown University Press, 2005.

Holmes, Augustine, OSB. *A Life Pleasing to God: The Spirituality of the Rules of St. Basil.* London: Darton, Longman & Todd, 2000.

Hudson, Winthrop S., ed. *Walter Rauschenbusch: Selected Writings.* Classics of Western Spirituality. Mahwah, NJ: Paulist Press, 1984.

Inge, Denise. *Happiness and Holiness: Thomas Traherne and His Writings.* Norwich, UK: Canterbury Press, 2008.

Isasi-Díaz, Ada María. *Mujerista Theology: A Theology for the 21st Century.* Maryknoll, NY: Orbis Books, 1996.

Jantzen, Grace. *Power, Gender and Christian Mysticism.* Cambridge: Cambridge University Press, 1995.

Johnson, Elizabeth. *She Who Is: The Mystery of God in Feminist Theological Discourse.* New York: Crossroad, 1996.

Johnston, William. *The Still Point: Reflections on Zen and Christian Mysticism.* New York: Fordham University Press, 1989.

Kadowaki, Kakichi. *Zen and the Bible.* Maryknoll, NY: Orbis Books, 2002.

Kardong, Terrence G., ed. *Benedict's Rule: A Translation and Commentary.* Collegeville, MN: Liturgical Press, 1996.

Kavanaugh, Kieran, ed. *John of the Cross: Selected Writings.* Classics of Western Spirituality. Mahwah, NJ: Paulist Press, 1987.

Kavanaugh, Kieran, and Rodriguez, Otilio, trans. *Teresa of Avila: The Interior Castle.* Classics of Western Spirituality. Mahwah, NJ: Paulist Press, 1979.

Keating, Thomas. *Open Mind, Open Heart: The Contemplative Dimension of the Gospel*. New York: Continuum, 1998.

Kelly, Geffrey B., and F. Burton Nelson. *The Cost of Moral Leadership: The Spirituality of Dietrich Bonhoeffer*. Grand Rapids, MI: Eerdmans, 2003.

Kim, Yung Suk, and Kim, Jin-Ho, eds. *Reading Minjung Theology in the Twenty-First Century*. Eugene, OR: Wipf and Stock, 2013.

Krey, Philip D. W., and Peter D. S. Krey, eds. and trans. *Luther's Spirituality*. Classics of Western Spirituality. Mahwah, NJ: Paulist Press, 2007.

Kwok Pui-Lan. *Postcolonial Imagination and Feminist Theology*. London: SCM Press, 2005.

LaCugna, Catherine M. *God for Us: The Trinity and Christian Life*. San Francisco: HarperCollins, 1993.

Lane, Belden. *The Solace of Fierce Landscapes: Exploring Desert and Mountain Spirituality*. New York: Oxford University Press, 1998.

Lawless, George. *Augustine of Hippo and His Monastic Rule*. Oxford: Clarendon Press, 1987.

Leclercq, Jean, OSB. *The Love of Learning and the Desire for God: A Study of Monastic Culture*, new ed. New York: Fordham University Press, 2003.

Liechty, Daniel, ed. and trans. *Early Anabaptist Spirituality*. Classics of Western Spirituality. Mahwah, NJ: Paulist Press, 1994.

Lonsdale, David. *Eyes to See, Ears to Hear: An Introduction to Ignatian Spirituality*. London: Darton, Longman & Todd, 2000.

Louth, Andrew. *The Origins of the Christian Mystical Tradition: From Plato to Denys*. Oxford: Clarendon Press, 1981.

———. *Theology and Spirituality*. Fairacres Publications 55. Oxford: SLG Press, 1978.

Luibheid, Colm, trans. *John Cassian: Conferences*. Classics of Western Spirituality. Mahwah, NJ: Paulist Press, 1985.

Luibheid, Colm, and Paul Rorem, trans. *Pseudo-Dionysius: The Complete Works*. Classics of Western Spirituality. Mahwah, NJ: Paulist Press, 1987.

Luibheid, Colm, and Norman Russell, trans. *John Climacus: The Ladder of Divine Ascent*. Classics of Western Spirituality. Mahwah, NJ: Paulist Press, 1982.

Main, John. *Word into Silence: A Manual of Christian Meditation*, new ed. Norwich, UK: Canterbury Press, 2006.

Martinez, Gaspar. *Confronting the Mystery of God: Political, Liberation and Public Theologies*. New York: Continuum, 2001.

McEntee, Rory, and Adam Bucko. *The New Monasticism: An Interspiritual Manifesto for Contemplative Living*. Maryknoll, NY: Orbis Books, 2015.

McGinn, Bernard. *The Foundations of Mysticism: Origins to the Fifth Century*. New York: Crossroad, 1991.

———. "The Letter and the Spirit: Spirituality as an Academic Discipline." In *Minding the Spirit: The Study of Christian Spirituality*, ed. Elizabeth Dreyer and Mark Burrows, 25–41. Baltimore, MD: Johns Hopkins University Press, 2005.

———. *The Mystical Thought of Meister Eckhart*. New York: Crossroad, 2001.

———. *Mysticism in the Reformation: 1500–1650, Part 1*. New York: Crossroad, 2016.

McGinn, Bernard, and Edmund Colledge, trans. *Meister Eckhart: The Essential Sermons, Commentaries, Treatises, and Defense*. Classics of Western Spirituality. Mahwah, NJ: Paulist Press, 1985.

McGinn, Bernard, and Frank Tobin, trans. *Meister Eckhart: Teacher and Preacher*. Classics of Western Spirituality. Mahwah, NJ: Paulist Press, 1987.

McGreal, Wilfrid. *At the Fountain of Elijah: The Carmelite Tradition*. London: Darton, Longman & Todd, 1999.

McGuckin, John. *Standing in God's Holy Fire: The Byzantine Tradition*. London: Darton, Longman & Todd, 2001.

McKee, Elsie Anne, ed. and trans. *John Calvin: Writings on Pastoral Piety*. Classics of Western Spirituality. Mahwah, NJ: Paulist Press, 2001.

Merton, Thomas. *Conjectures of a Guilty Bystander*. New York: Doubleday, 1966.

———. *Contemplative Prayer*. London: Darton, Longman & Todd, 1973.

———. *Life and Holiness*. New York: Doubleday Image, 1964.

———. *A Vow of Conversation: Journals 1964–65*, ed. Naomi Button Stone. New York: Farrar Strauss Giroux, 1988.

Meyendorff, John, ed., Nicholas Gendle, trans. *Gregory Palamas: The Triads*. Classics of Western Spirituality. Mahwah, NJ: Paulist Press, 1983.

Miles, Margaret R. *Practicing Christianity: Critical Perspectives for an Embodied Spirituality*. New York: Crossroad, 1988.

Moltmann, Jürgen. *Experiences of God*. Philadelphia: Fortress Press, 1980.

Munitiz, Joseph, and Philip Endean, eds. *Saint Ignatius of Loyola: Personal Writings*. London: Penguin Books, 1996.

Noffke, Suzanne, trans. *Catherine of Siena: The Dialogue*. Classics of Western Spirituality. Mahwah, NJ: Paulist Press, 1980.

Oduyoye, Mercy Amba. *Beads and Strands: Reflections of an African Woman on Christianity in Africa*. Maryknoll, NY: Orbis Books, 2004.

Orchard, Helen, ed. *Spirituality in Health Care Contexts*. London: Jessica Kingsley, 2001.

Panofsky, Erwin. *Abbot Suger on the Abbey Church of St. Denis and Its Art Treasures*, 2nd ed. Princeton, NJ: Princeton University Press, 1979.

Pentkovsky, Aleksei, ed. *The Pilgrim's Tale*. Classics of Western Spirituality. Mahwah, NJ: Paulist Press, 1999.

Raguin, Virginia Chieffo, Kathryn Brush, and Peter Draper, eds. *Artistic Integration in Gothic Buildings*. Toronto: University of Toronto Press, 1995.

Raitt, Jill, ed. *Christian Spirituality II: High Middle Ages and Reformation*. World Spirituality. New York: Crossroad, 1987.

Rajkumar, Peniel. *Dalit Theology and Dalit Liberation*. Farnham, UK: Ashgate, 2010.

Randall, Ian. *What a Friend We Have in Jesus: The Evangelical Tradition*. London: Darton, Longman & Todd, 2005.

Rowell, Geoffrey, Kenneth Stevenson, and Rowan Williams, eds. *Love's Redeeming Work: The Anglican Quest for Holiness*. Oxford: Oxford University Press, 2001.

Rowland, Christopher, ed. *The Cambridge Companion to Liberation Theology*. Cambridge: Cambridge University Press, 2007.

Ruffing, Janet, ed. *Mysticism and Social Transformation*. Syracuse, NY: Syracuse University Press, 2001.

Ryan, Frances, and John Rybolt, eds. *Vincent de Paul and Louise de Marillac: Rules, Conferences, and Writings*. Classics of Western Spirituality. Mahwah, NJ: Paulist Press, 1995.

Schneiders, Sandra. "Approaches to the Study of Christian Spirituality." In *The Blackwell Companion to Christian Spirituality*, ed. Arthur Holder, 15–33. Malden, MA: Blackwell, 2005.

———. *The Revelatory Text: Interpreting the New Testament as Sacred Scripture*. Collegeville, MN: Liturgical Press, 1999.

———. "The Study of Christian Spirituality: Contours and Dynamics of a Discipline." In *Minding the Spirit: The Study of Christian Spirituality*, ed. Elizabeth Dreyer and Mark Burrows, 5–24. Baltimore, MD: Johns Hopkins University Press, 2005.

Schwanda, Tom. *Soul Recreation: The Contemplative-Mystical Piety of Puritanism*. Eugene, OR: Wipf and Stock, 2012.

Sheldrake, Philip. *Explorations in Spirituality: History, Theology and Social Practice*. Mahwah, NJ: Paulist Books, 2010.

———, ed. *Heaven in Ordinary: George Herbert and His Writings*. London: Canterbury Press, 2009.

———. *Julian of Norwich: "In God's Sight"—Her Theology in Context*. Oxford: Wiley-Blackwell, 2018.

———. *Living Between Worlds: Place and Journey in Celtic Spirituality*, 2nd ed. London: Darton, Longman & Todd, 1997.

———, ed. *The New SCM Dictionary of Christian Spirituality*. London: SCM Press, 2005.

———, ed. *The New Westminster Dictionary of Christian Spirituality*. Louisville, KY: Westminster John Knox Press, 2005.

———. *Spaces for the Sacred: Place Memory and Identity*. London: SCM Press, 2001.

———. *The Spiritual City: Theology, Spirituality and the Urban*. Oxford: Wiley-Blackwell, 2014.

———. *Spirituality: A Brief History*, 2nd ed. Oxford: Wiley-Blackwell, 2013.

———. *Spirituality: A Guide for the Perplexed*. London: Bloomsbury, 2014.

———. *Spirituality and History: Questions of Interpretation and Method*, rev. ed. Maryknoll, NY: Orbis Books, 1998.

———. *Spirituality and Theology: Christian Living and the Doctrine of God*. Maryknoll, NY: Orbis Books, 1999.

———. *Spirituality: A Very Short Introduction*. Oxford: Oxford University Press, 2012.

Shrady, Maria, trans. *Johannes Tauler: Sermons*. Classics of Western Spirituality. Mahwah, NJ: Paulist Press, 1985.

Snyder, C. Arnold. *Following in the Footsteps of Christ: The Anabaptist Tradition*. London: Darton, Longman & Todd, 2004.

Sobrino, Jon. *Spirituality of Liberation: Towards Political Holiness*. Maryknoll, NY: Orbis Books, 1988.

Sobrino, Jon, and Ignacio Ellacuría, eds. *Systematic Theology: Perspectives from Liberation Theology*. Maryknoll, NY: Orbis Books, 1996.

Stanwood, Paul, ed. *William Law: A Serious Call to a Devout and Holy Life, The Spirit of Love*. Classics of Western Spirituality. Mahwah, NJ: Paulist Press, 1978.

Stewart, Columba, OSB. *Prayer and Community: The Benedictine Tradition*. Traditions of Christian Spirituality. London: Darton, Longman & Todd, 1998.

Thibert, Péronne Marie, trans. *Francis de Sales, Jane de Chantal: Letters of Spiritual Direction*. Classics of Western Spirituality. Mahwah, NJ: Paulist Press, 1988.

Thompson, William, ed., Lowell Glendon, trans. *Bérulle and the French School: Selected Writings*. Classics of Western Spirituality. Mahwah, NJ: Paulist Press, 1989.

Tobin, Frank, ed. and trans. *Henry Suso: The Exemplar, with Two German Sermons*. Classics of Western Spirituality. Mahwah, NJ: Paulist Press, 1989.

———. trans. *Mechthild of Magdeburg: The Flowing Light of the Godhead*. Classics of Western Spirituality. Mahwah, NJ: Paulist Press, 1998.

Tracy, David. *The Analogical Imagination: Christian Theology and the Culture of Pluralism*. New York: Crossroad, 1991.

———. *Blessed Rage for Order*. New York: Seabury Press, 1975.

———. *On Naming the Present: God, Hermeneutics and Church*. Maryknoll, NY: Orbis Books, 1994.

Traherne, Thomas. *Centuries*. London: Mowbray, 1975.

———. *Selected Poems and Prose*. London: Penguin Books, 1991.

Underhill, Evelyn. *Mysticism: The Nature and Development of Spiritual Consciousness*. Oxford: Oneworld, 1993.

Van Engen, John, trans. *Devotio Moderna: Basic Writings*. Classics of Western Spirituality. Mahwah, NJ: Paulist Press, 1988.

Villa-Vicencio, Charles. *A Theology of Reconstruction: Nation-Building and Human Rights*. Cambridge: Cambridge University Press, 1992.

Villa-Vicencio, Charles, and John W. de Gruchy, eds. *Resistance and Hope: South African Essays in Honour of Beyers Naude*. Grand Rapids, MI: Eerdmans, 1985.

Vivian, Tim. *Journeying into God: Seven Early Monastic Lives*. Minneapolis: Fortress Press, 1996.

Waaijman, Kees. *Spirituality: Forms, Foundations, Methods*. Leuven, Belgium: Peeters, 2002.

Ward, Benedicta, trans. *The Desert Fathers: Sayings of the Early Christian Monks*. London: Penguin Books, 2003.

————, ed. *The Wisdom of the Desert Fathers*. Oxford: Fairacres, 1986.

Whaling, Frank, ed. *John and Charles Wesley: Selected Prayers, Hymns, Journal Notes, Sermons, Letters and Treatises*. Classics of Western Spirituality. Mahwah, NJ: Paulist Press, 1981.

Williams, Rowan. *The Wound of Knowledge*. London: Darton, Longman & Todd, 1990.

Wilson, Christopher. *The Gothic Cathedral*. London: Thames & Hudson, 1990.

Winkworth, Margaret, trans. and ed. *Gertrude of Helfta: The Herald of Divine Love*. Classics of Western Spirituality. Mahwah, NJ: Paulist Press, 1993.

Wiseman, James, trans. *John Ruusbroec: The Spiritual Espousals and Other Works*. Classics of Western Spirituality. Mahwah, NJ: Paulist Press, 1985.

Wright, Wendy. *Heart Speaks to Heart: The Salesian Tradition*. London: Darton, Longman & Todd, 2004.

Woods, Richard, and Peter Tyler, eds. *The Bloomsbury Guide to Christian Spirituality*. London: Bloomsbury, 2012.

Index